BEGINNERS' BOOK OF BEAUTIFUL FOOD

BEGINNERS' BOOK OF
BEAUTIFUL
FOOD

IRENA CHALMERS

AND THE EDITORS OF
BRIDE'S

ILLUSTRATIONS BY MEL KLAPHOLZ

DOUBLEDAY & COMPANY, INC.
GARDEN CITY, NEW YORK
1976

DESIGNED BY LAURENCE ALEXANDER

Library of Congress Cataloging in Publication Data
Chalmers, Irena.
Beginners' book of beautiful food.

Includes index.
1. Cookery.   I. Bride's.   II. Title.
TX715.C446   641.5
ISBN: 0-385-11097-9
Library of Congress Catalog Card Number: 76-2762
Copyright © 1976 by The Condé Nast Publications Inc.

For Hilary and Philip,
with love

CONTENTS

INTRODUCTION

There are endless tales told about young brides who boiled their first egg until it exploded, or forgot to turn the oven on only to discover an hour later, when all the guests were seated, that the chicken was still sitting there, smiling smugly, innocent and plump, and completely, horrifyingly raw. Well, that will not happen to you. Good cooking is largely a state of mind, and if you want to be a great cook, you undoubtedly will be.

I have always held the firm though not very original belief that if you can read you can cook. You can even make some quite splendid dishes without cooking at all, simply by assembling a group of fresh foods into a glorious salad full of peaks and valleys of taste, texture and contrasts.

Learning how to cook is just a matter of understanding a few logical rules. After all, no matter how complicated a recipe may seem, it is only possible to cook the food by a process of roasting, frying, broiling, or boiling. (Baking, deep-fat frying, and poaching are just variations of these techniques.) However, it is important to know when to use one method of cooking rather than another; why tough meat should be stewed and tender meat fried or broiled. It is of equal importance to know which are the tough and tender meats. If you are following a recipe slavishly, without understanding the personality of the ingredients, or knowing exactly what you are doing and why, it is almost impossible to know when the fish is ready, when to turn the steak, and why a sauce that separates and curdles on one occasion turns into a culinary triumph on another.

It is extremely liberating to feel you are master of your own kitchen. When you are able to sense the idea behind a recipe, and recognize the existence of common denominators within a group of ingredients, you can then relate an unfamiliar preparation to a whole family of dishes. At this point, you will be able to see, as you face an awesome-looking page of print, that a recipe for curried beef is simply a beef stew with curry and yoghurt added, while a goulash is the original beef stew but with the addition of paprika and sour cream. All stews follow the same pattern of cooking, but the addition or deletion of a few ingredients makes each dish appear to be entirely different from all other dishes. When you are able to reduce the concept of a recipe to its simplest terms, cooking becomes easier, quicker, and you can become more inventive.

As you add your own ideas to established recipes, it is important to know when one ingredient may safely be substituted for another or even omitted entirely. A broiled chuck steak will not prove a satisfactory alternative to porterhouse because chuck is a fibrous, fatty cut of meat and tastes much better if it is cooked in liquid for a long period of time. On the other hand, some ingredients can be interchanged very successfully; as an example, chicken is a good substitute for veal; cornstarch can be used as a thickening instead of flour; and three egg yolks can safely be used to replace two whole eggs.

Different cooking methods will produce entirely different dishes from the same group of ingredients. For instance, the identical ingredients, used in identical proportions, can be made into a custard sauce, the filling for a pie, or frozen into ice cream. This same combination—eggs, sugar, milk, and vanilla—forms one step in the preparation of a Bavarian cream, a mousse, and a rice pudding.

In the beginning there seem to be many lengthy chores in the kitchen that take up an interminable length of time. Chopping is one of those techniques that, until you have acquired the necessary skill, take so maddeningly long you are tempted to buy only packaged frozen onions. Acquiring a new skill is like learning how to serve a tennis ball or play the violin, and the only way to do it well is to practice over and over again. What a dreary admonition, but one that really works. Fortunately, as you will probably be making at least one meal a day for the next many years, there will be plenty of opportunity to become an expert, and eventually you will become an artist as well as an artisan.

There are few things that give greater joy than selecting from the abundance of the good earth. The delight of discovering the first slim tender stalks of asparagus can be matched only by the sensual pleasure of eating them. What can compare with the satisfaction of bringing home baskets of tomatoes bursting with summer red ripeness, fruits and berries warmed by the heat of the sun? Tiny new potatoes, peas snuggling in crisp pods are irresistible accompaniments conjuring up visions of roast lamb or poached salmon with a sumptuous bowl of hollandaise sauce.

Cooking with the constant renewal of the seasons brings fresh delights to your kitchen, and as month merges into month, your menus reflect the progress of the year. The choices are limitless, bounded only by your own enthusiasm, and the rewards for time well spent are their own justification.

⤳ EQUIPPING THE KITCHEN ⤶

We cannot overestimate the influence of the past on our contemporary way of life. Though it may seem a far step from cooking in an old iron caldron to preparing dinner in a modern electric slow cooker, both utensils solve a problem in society as it is constructed at a particular point in history. The caldron and the slow cooker enable the cook to perform a variety of other tasks while the evening meal is cooking by itself without constant attention.

Cooking is a craft as well as a science and an art, and cooks, like craftsmen, must have the correct tools to be able to work efficiently. It is a source of continuing fascination to me to watch other people at work, and my mind reels at the variety of their range of tools. Compare the delicacy of the instruments of an eye surgeon with those of an orthopedic or thoracic surgeon. Look at the many gadgets used by a plumber, an automobile mechanic, a piano tuner, a photographer, or an aerospace scientist. Each profession, each trade, each craft equips itself with tools that have a specific and clearly defined purpose. Each piece of equipment is designed to fulfill only that single operation, and though in an emergency one tool may be substituted for another, the loss of the correct tool will certainly make the task more difficult and the result may not be as good.

So it is, or should be, with tools for cooking. There is no more fundamentally important work than cooking, yet many people take years and years to equip their kitchen and sacrifice the opportunity to buy good equipment that would make their lives far easier, in order to have some striped wallpaper or a new carpet.

Do not feel guilty about buying the very best of cooking utensils. They will last a lifetime and will not only give you infinite pleasure and satisfaction, but will enable you to do the job easily and efficiently rather than making it more difficult. I am sure I have made a thousand omelettes in my life, but I can assure you that if I had to use a new pan from the five-and-ten-cent store the omelette would be a disaster and I would be totally unable to convince you that I am really good at making omelettes!

A professional cook would never spare valuable space in the kitchen for equipment that merely looked pretty but did not serve a function efficiently. Buy only those utensils that you really need and those that are the best possible quality. If you cannot afford the very best equipment at one time, add one good pot at a time rather than settling for a poor imitation of the real thing.

POTS AND PANS

Utensils for cooking over direct heat on top of the stove or in the oven must be made of heavy metal. A heavy pan will distribute the heat evenly and food will not stick and burn on the bottom of the pan. Lids must fit tightly or juices and liquids will evaporate and escape from the pan in the form of steam, leaving the food dry and tasteless. If, on the other hand, the steam condenses on the inner surface of the lid, it will fall back into the pan, bathing the food with moisture.

Select the size of pan to accommodate the food snugly. For example, if you cook a chicken in a casserole that is too small, the chicken will be squashed and uncomfortable, and the inside will cook unevenly while the parts that are touching the hot metal will become dry and burnt. There should be just enough space that the chicken will be content to sit in a natural position. If you put it in too large a pan, a greater surface area will be exposed. It will feel overwhelmed by the space and cook too quickly with a rapid evaporation of the juices.

The best materials for saucepans and casseroles are tin- or steel-lined copper, though these pans have become so costly they are beyond the reach of all but the most dedicatedly serious cooks. The next best thing is enameled iron followed by stainless steel and heavy aluminum. I cannot stress too strongly the importance of avoiding lightweight saucepans. They are far more trouble than they are worth. Milk and sauces will scorch and boil over the second you turn your back, and apart from the sheer waste of the ingredients, the pans are difficult to clean and easily dented and chipped. If you already own such potential saboteurs, throw them out or spray-paint the outside and use them for plant pots.

Casseroles should be made of flame-resistant material so they can be taken from the oven and put directly on top of a burner. China, earthenware, and clay casseroles cannot be used in this way or they will break. Metal casseroles are more practical because sauces can be adjusted on top of the stove without having to use an additional saucepan. It is also quicker to reheat food on top of the stove rather than in the oven.

FRYING PANS

Frying pans should, like saucepans, be made of heavy material: tin- or steel-lined copper, enameled iron, heavy aluminum, or stainless steel. Teflon coverings are continually being improved, and some types of Teflon can even be attacked with sharp instruments without causing damage, though the manufacturers do not recommend you actually put their product to a practical test. Teflon pans are easy to clean, and the claim is made that Teflon prevents the food from sticking to the pan. This is true, but food will not stick to other good quality materials either, and Teflon not only tends to wear out eventually, but initially increases the over-all cost of the pan.

Frying pans should be shallow so there can be a rapid evaporation of steam. If the steam condenses in the pan, the fat becomes waterlogged and the food will stew in its own juices rather than fry and become a good brown color. Handles should be made of wood or heat-resistant material so you do not have to reach constantly for a pot holder. The handles should be angled away from the pan and be long enough that they extend beyond the flame. Test the balance of the frying pan by tilting it backward and forward to see if it feels comfortable in your hand. You will need at least two frying pans: a small one for frying two eggs, a few mushrooms, or other small quantity of food, and a larger one for cooking bacon, chops, and for poaching fish.

KNIVES

Imagine you are on a deserted island and you can only have one piece of cooking equipment. You will surely be able to fashion a clay pot or cook on hot stones, but you must have a chef's knife with an eight-inch blade. You will be able to keep and maintain a sharp edge if the blade of the knife is made of carbon steel, and it can be used to replace dozens of gadgets that are normally found in the kitchen. You can cut up a chicken, remove the bone from a leg of lamb, clean a passing fish, chop, mince, cut, or slice any and all fruits and vegetables. A good sharp knife is an absolutely essential piece of equipment.

Carbon steel will stain when it is used for cutting onions and citrus fruits, but it can be cleaned easily by rubbing it gently with scouring powder. Dry the knife immediately or it will rust, and do not put it in the dishwasher or it will become spotted with the detergent and be more diffi-cult to clean. This sounds as though cleaning carbon steel is quite an effort, but it is not really, and the small amount of care that is required is willingly given because it performs its function so well. (Some people choose stainless steel rather than carbon because stainless does not need any care at all. However, it is impossible to obtain as sharp an edge as with carbon steel, and even if you could prove this statement wrong, devotees of carbon steel would never be convinced you were right. The controversy is one that has raged for years and is probably insoluble because each school of thought holds rigidly to its own opinion.)

For the sake of convenience, I find stainless steel to be entirely satis-factory and practical for a second knife, a 3½" or 4" blade paring knife. These two knives, the chef's knife and the paring knife, are all you need for the foundation of the kitchen. Other knives, such as a ham slicer and a carving knife, a boning knife and a serrated-edge knife for cutting bread and tomatoes, are helpful to have but not essential.

A wooden chopping block does the least damage to sharp knives and is aesthetically more pleasing than any other material.

WHISKS

Whisks have roughly equal importance to knives. You can manage with a 10″ whisk in the beginning and add smaller and larger sizes as you feel you need them. Whisks guarantee that all your sauces will be smooth and free from lumps and other miseries.

OMELETTE AND CREPE PANS

These two pans come under the heading of special equipment. Though they are not essential to the survival of the human race, you cannot make omelettes or crepes without the right pan or they will stick and cause you terrible embarrassment. See omelette and crepe chapters on how to season the pan.

WOK

A wok has the most perfect design of all cooking utensils. Its shape is ideally fitted to its function. The wide flaring sides conduct the heat evenly and rapidly to make an extremely large cooking surface, enabling food to be stir-fried rapidly without losing contact with the source of heat. The food is cooked so quickly it retains its fresh taste, firm texture, and nutritional value. The wok is easy to handle and with the use of a lid can be adapted for braising, steaming, and even poaching. The stir-frying method of cooking is a marvelously efficient way of making a quick dinner and stretching small quantities of food into a satisfying meal. The exact combinations of ingredients need never be the same, so with a wok in the kitchen you can constantly create new harmonious blends and contrasts of taste and texture.

FRENCH FRYER

We are straying away now from the absolutely basic essentials and moving into the area of "I wish I had a . . ." category. A French fryer will make it possible to cook fried foods so they will be crisp and crunchy on the outside and succulently moist on the inside. To achieve this miracle of perfection will involve a ten- or fifteen-dollar investment, but it is worth every penny. The inner basket of the fryer permits all the food to be lifted out of the fat at one time, the food is suspended above the fat to drain and then returned to the piping-hot fat for a second immersion, at which time it becomes firm and brown. This two-process method of frying is superior in every way to the alternative of leaving the food to fry in fat that is declining in heat. The temperature of the cooking fat always falls when cold raw food is added, so it is necessary to remove the food after the initial cooking period and reheat the fat to the correct frying temperature of 375°.

ICE-CREAM MAKERS

The small electric ice-cream makers are very convenient for making one quart of ice cream. There is no need to crush the ice as in the customary method of making a larger quantity of ice cream, for this gadget fits neatly in the freezer compartment of the refrigerator and literally makes the ice cream by itself.

THE ELECTRIC SLOW COOKER

The slow cookers or crock-pot (tm) by any other name are a great convenience if you are out of the home all day. The food cooks at 200°, it costs only three cents to cook an entire meal, and the convenience and pleasure of arriving home to find a tender roast chicken or a hot soup or stew waiting for you are immeasurable.

THE MICROWAVE OVEN

The microwave oven is an extremely expensive convenience. It does not perform any cooking process better than other standard kitchen equipment, but it certainly does it faster. A luxury indeed.

FOOD PROCESSOR

This is a combination mixer, blender, food chopper, slicer, and grater. It replaces many other gadgets in the kitchen. The initial cost is great but so are its convenience and efficiency.

❧ THE BASIC NECESSITIES ☙

For Cutting, Slicing, Chopping, and Carving

8″ chef's knife
4″ paring knife
13″ serrated-edge knife for cutting bread
Kitchen fork
Chopping block 20″ x 15″ x 1¾″

For Cooking

1½-quart casserole
4-quart casserole
1-quart saucepan with tightly fitting lid
3-quart saucepan with tightly fitting lid

French fryer
9" cake pan
2 baking sheets
Baking pan 13" x 9" x 2"
2 loaf tins 8½" x 4½" x 2½"
Wire cooling rack
12" frying pan
8" frying pan

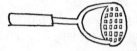

For Preparation

10" wire whisk
9½" wooden spatula
Rubber spatula
Potato peeler
Potato masher
Tongs
Grater
Kitchen scissors
Slotted kitchen spoon
Serving spoon
Small strainer
Large strainer
Pastry blender
Rolling pin
Small pancake turner
Large pancake turner
Colander
Custard cups
3 bowls
Rotary mixer
Can opener
Bottle opener
Coffee maker
Toaster
Oven mitts
Trivets
Pepper mill

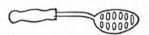

❧ TO BE ACQUIRED ❧
AS SOON AS POSSIBLE

Carving knife and fork
Serrated tomato knife
Grapefruit knife
14″ wire whisk
14″ wooden spatula
Molds, e.g., 1½-quart mold
Individual and 1-quart, 1½- and 2-quart soufflé dishes
Ramekins
Scallop shells
Pie plates 5″ and 7″
Spring form cake pan 8¾″
Square baking pan 8″ x 8″
Ladles large and small
Melon-ball maker
Egg slicer
Nutmeg grater
Cherry pitter
Apple corer
Juice maker
Large coffeepot
Electric mixer
Blender
Meat grinder
2-quart saucepan with tightly fitting lid
4-quart saucepan with tightly fitting lid
14″ frying pan
Waffle iron
Ice-cream maker
Ice-cream scoop
Omelette pan
Crepe pan
Wok
Chinese cleaver
Food processor
Microwave oven

≫ EATING AND DINING ≪

I think it can be said that there are two parallel styles of cooking. One involves eating, and the other dining. Those who merely eat do not buy TV dinners because they necessarily think they taste good, but because they do not know how to assemble a meal quickly and without effort. They feel uneasy in the kitchen and, not knowing exactly what they are doing, nor why ingredients appear to behave unpredictably, they do not feel their time will be well spent. As a consequence, they shrug off the whole subject saying they are not interested or are too busy to bother. (Though, interestingly, these same people are happy, even delighted, to go to a good restaurant and linger for two or three hours over dinner.)

I suspect, though I do not know for sure, that those who cannot cook spend considerably more money and time on eating than those who can prepare their own meals. Nobody is born with the ability to cook, but the knowledge can be acquired with the help of a few reliable books and a certain amount of practice and experience. After a while it is possible to dispense with almost all printed recipes, except perhaps to check the exact proportions of an ingredient or two.

This may seem like a utopian idea, but if you know how to make one omelette, a basic soufflé, or a stew, you can make them all and it just becomes a question of adding or substituting a few ingredients. The method of cooking whole families of dishes remains the same.

There is a tendency when you are deeply interested in any subject to suppose that others are missing something if they do not share your own pleasure. Yet I think food is a subject apart from all other hobbies and interests. It is both a private and public pleasure, and if only the word "gourmet" could be stricken from our language, we could dispense with all the elitisms that surround the whole field of eating and drinking wine, and be far more relaxed about just preparing good things to eat. Even with very limited funds and a small supply of ingredients there are many potential endings from the same beginning. For instance, suppose you had only six ingredients; a chicken, butter, flour, milk, one herb, and eggs, look how many meals you could make:

Roast Chicken	Chicken Pot Pie
Broiled Chicken	Chicken Kiev
Braised Chicken	Chicken Breasts with Sauce
Chicken Stew	Supreme
Chicken Soup	Southern Batter-Fried Chicken
Chicken Omelette	Chicken Croquettes
Chicken Soufflé	Chicken-Filled "Cream Puffs" for
Chicken Crepes	Hors d'Oeuvres
	Etc.

The list is endless but this is sufficient to emphasize the point that, having mastered the fundamental techniques of cooking, you are no longer doomed to eating the same things all the time. Imagine what you can conjure up if you have more than six ingredients. You can indeed dine, not merely eat.

❧ SHOPPING ❧

It is not possible or even desirable to be absolutely sensible every minute of the day, but you will save a great deal of time and vast sums of money if you do a little planning before you go shopping. Today food is costing between 20 and 30 per cent of an average family's consumer budget, so it is essential to spend the money wisely to obtain the maximum benefit from each dollar.

Before you pass through the doors of the supermarket to face all the array of brightly colored packages, have a clear idea of how many meals you are planning to serve. If you are buying for four days, decide in advance if you are going to have one meat, one chicken, one fish, and one meatless dinner or whatever combination that would be satisfactory. Then buy the principal ingredient, the meat or fish, first.

Be ruthlessly realistic about both the money and the time you have available. Bear in mind that you are probably going to be quite tired if you have been working all day. Know your own limitations. No matter how much you think you should make an economical little casserole, consider whether you really will carry out your good intentions. Otherwise wait until the weekend to prepare dishes that require a long cooking period.

This may seem pretty elementary, but if you come home to find only those ingredients that will take hours to be ready for the table, you may decide to scrap the whole idea of cooking and go out for dinner. This not only destroys the budget, but the food that you bought originally may eventually be wasted. It would then have been better to buy a more expensive meat that takes only a few minutes to cook.

Plan the main courses around seasonally adjusted prices. Though pork may be a bargain one week, beef may be a better buy the following week. The prices are constantly fluctuating, so you have to keep paying attention to the variations in the costs. Experiment with new foods as though you were away on vacation. Some foods for which there is not a great demand are surprisingly inexpensive, and often the only reason for the low price is that people do not know how to cook them. Try a fish you have never had before and you may well find that you enjoy it as much as a more familiar but more expensive fish. But do not buy for the sake of economy only. If deep down you have a suspicious feeling that you will never learn to love kidneys or hearts or bird brains, do not buy them merely because they cost less than sirloin steak. There is little chance that there will be a fundamental change in your opinion as soon as you get them home. They will just sit there doggedly in the refrigerator until with relief you can throw them out because they have gone bad.

It is a good idea to restrain an impulsive enthusiasm for a new food, though, until your next trip to the supermarket. In the meantime look it up in a cookbook and buy all the other ingredients that will be needed to complete the recipe. By buying foods that are always inexpensive, you will ultimately save far more than shopping for bargains among the higher-priced meats and produce.

When you have narrowed down your choice to a single meat, the decisions are not yet over. It is necessary to decide whether it is wiser to buy meat without a bone that is more expensive than meat with a bone. You are, of course, paying something for the weight of the bone, which will be thrown away, unless it is used for soup. The higher-priced meat will yield more servings per pound and may ultimately be more economical than the less expensive cut.

The quality of the meat is also important. Inexpensive ground chuck contains a high proportion of fat and the meat shrinks to a smaller quantity than the more costly ground round. Tough meats can be marinated until they are tender, and chicken is less costly if you cut it up yourself. If you do not know how to cut it, ask the butcher if you can watch him. He will probably be delighted and, unless you ask him on Saturday afternoon, he will also show you how to bone it. It is much easier to see these things than to read about them.

A chicken in parts is an economical treasure house. You can serve the boned breasts with a cream sauce one night, and fry the legs another night. The back and wings become the base for chicken soup, the giblets are made into a sauce, the liver is saved and frozen until you have sufficient to make a chicken liver omelette, and if you are clever enough to find the feathers, you can make a hat.

Check the newspaper for special prices and keep constantly in mind the fact that you really have worked very hard for the money you are spending on food. Remember that every step you take yourself in the preparation of the meal will reduce its ultimate cost. Pay attention to unit pricing, which will show you the cost per serving.

It is very easy to succumb to convenience foods if you shop when you are hungry. The packages look so beautiful, yet most of them take at least half an hour to defrost and during that time you could have made an omelette or cooked a chop that would undoubtedly taste better and be more satisfying. Almost anything you make at home will taste better than reheated packaged frozen food.

If you are shopping in an unfamiliar neighborhood, try several super-markets before settling on the one you like best. Your favorite store may not have the lowest prices but be the one that is cleanest, where the food is freshest, and be the most pleasant one in which to shop. Unless you have unlimited time and are a passionate bargain hunter, it is best not to wander from store to store but remain faithful to one. You will find it more efficient and less effort to shop at one place all the time because you will know where everything is quickly and receive prompt attention if you have an occasional special request to make.

Use all the coupons and discount slips that are available. Many weekend specials are posted on Thursdays, and the earlier you shop the more likely you are to find the foods still available, and also be able to avoid the crowds.

Compare the prices, weights, and contents of the store's privately labeled canned foods and staples. They are almost always less expensive than brand names. Unless you plan to use a large quantity of bargain priced foods, stick to the smaller sizes, or the bargain may become a costly waste. But large boxes of cereal cost less than smaller sizes, vegetables, sugar, flour, and rice are less costly when they are packaged in bags rather than fancy boxes, so if you know you are going to eat them anyway, these foods are worth buying in bulk.

Look at some recipes before you make up a shopping list and have a fairly clear idea what you are going to buy, but at the same time keep an open mind. If a recipe calls for fresh mushrooms and the mushrooms do not look fresh, or it is the wrong season for mushrooms, do not hesitate to substitute another fresh vegetable or leave them out of the recipe entirely. They will not change the basic composition of the dish.

Buy only fresh vegetables in season, not only because they are less expensive when there is a plentiful supply, but because they also taste better and are nutritionally more sound when they have fully ripened in the sun. For the same reasons try to buy local fruits and vegetables. You would not think of importing your Brussels sprouts from Belgium or London, but California may be two thousand miles away from where you live, too, and somebody has to pay for the transportation costs. Do not hesitate either to ask for information about the food you buy in the supermarket. Your wisest investment is in the mutual respect you establish with the butcher and produce clerk. This does not mean you have to buy in large quantities or only the most expensive items in the store; you only have to be interested and be a regular customer.

If you do not know if a peach or avocado is ripe, look up the tests for ripeness further on in this book, or ask somebody who does know. If you resort to squeezing it, you will bruise and spoil it. It is also better, if possible, to buy loose vegetables and fruit. Not only is it extremely difficult to know what is lying beneath the shrink-wrapped packages, but you are also forced to pay for the packaging as well as having to buy a quantity and size the supermarket management decided you needed, rather than what you think you need. It is wise to buy only that quantity of fresh produce that you can reasonably expect to eat within three or four days.

Remember, too, that a large size does not necessarily indicate a proportionally greater virtue. Small tomatoes and eggplants are usually sweeter and more flavorful than those with a six-inch diameter.

It may be more economical to double the quantity of food that you buy with the idea of freezing half or saving the remainder for a second meal. Each of these decisions must be made on the basis of your knowledge of cooking. The more familiar you become with the various techniques of cooking, the greater the number of options you will have in your head when you are choosing which foods to buy. If you know how to make a good meal from leftovers, you are way ahead because you will know which other ingredients to buy and how long it will take to put everything together. If you forget an ingredient and have to shop two nights in a row, you not only waste the time you could be using for something else, but, unless you are very strong, you will end up buying magazines, coffeecakes, smoked oysters, and all manner of other little luxuries that, had you stayed out of the market, you would have avoided.

When you shop for dairy products, brown eggs are sometimes less costly than white, though there is no difference between them other than the color of the shell. Medium and small eggs are not as expensive as large eggs and are perfectly splendid for breakfast, though it is tricky trying to figure out how many small eggs to use when a recipe calls for six eggs and assumes you are using six large eggs. (A Grade A large egg weighs two ounces so you can work out the equation from that.) Cheese in bulk is less expensive than sliced cheese and remains moist for longer; nonfat dried milk is less costly than whole milk, and evaporated skimmed milk is more economical than evaporated whole milk. Butter in a one-pound block is several pennies less than individually wrapped quarters, and the extra quantity can be frozen.

There are a great many things to keep in mind as you stroll along the aisles, but they are mostly just common sense, and after a while you will be buying with increasing confidence.

⊱ BUYING MEAT ⊰

Clever shoppers are able to discover out-of-the-way places to buy clothes without the manufacturer's label, furniture with just a tiny scratch, and electrical appliances below the usual retail price. When you are buying meat there are no such bargains. Meat must have a prime or choice label, or it has to be regarded with the deepest suspicion. Though the design of an article of clothing can be copied and made with less costly fabric and minor attention to detail, the costs of feeding, breeding, and raising animals do not have any area for short cuts. The only bargains that are available are in the method of buying and selling.

Meats bought through a community co-operative plan cost less than those where there is a higher overhead and the selling costs have to be included in the final price. Meat bought directly from a butcher in a butcher's shop almost always costs more than meat from a supermarket. However, it is important to remember that comparing the costs of meats is like comparing apples and pears. Supermarket meat is not necessarily the same quality as butcher-shop meat. You may arrive home with two pounds of ground chuck from one place that will be full of fat and shrink when it is cooked, yet two pounds of ground chuck from another place will yield a greater amount of cooked meat. While the two packages appear to be identical, one may cost more because the chuck from one store is of finer quality than from the other. Your meat dollar tends to be a classic example of that old cliché "He who laughs last . . ."

You can make a naturally tough cut of good quality meat tender and delicious by cooking it well, but though you may add meat tenderizers and flavor enhancers to poor quality meat, you will inevitably end up with a tasteless, flabby piece of meat no matter how hard you try to make it into something it is not.

Buy the best meat you can afford, and if the budget is very tightly stretched, make do with smaller portions and fill out the meal by making one of the many quickly prepared hot breads or serve an additional fresh vegetable. Good meat, even in small quantities, is more satisfying than a larger amount of tasteless meat. It may also be wise to have some completely meatless meals and serve a good homemade soup and dessert rather than a more formal meal at least one night a week.

The fashions or style of eating is constantly changing, and we are increasingly being influenced by social, political, and economic factors over which we have little control. Anthropologists claim that our origins lay in foraging vegetarianism, and we changed our diet only over an incalculable period of time to become meat eaters. Though we read historical accounts of vast orgies of food, the sheer quantity would be impossible for us to contemplate today. In fact we cannot even eat as much meat as our immediate ancestors. This is probably quite a good thing, though. There seem to be as many people in affluent societies who suffer from eating too much as those who eat too little. We have great freedom to choose what we eat, so it does seem a little foolish to squander money on food wrappings rather than the food itself. When you buy a frozen chicken pot pie, it does not appear to cost very much at all, but as your fork fishes around in a sea of pea- and carrot-dotted cornstarch sauce for the odd piece of chicken promised by the photograph on the box, you begin to grasp why it is that, if you make a chicken pot pie at home, yours will cost more and take longer to prepare. But compare the results, and if you still choose a frozen pot pie you cannot complain that you are tired, because you are not receiving adequate nutrition, nor that you are becoming overweight, because you ate all that starchy food.

All this is a preamble to saying that I hope this guide will help you select food to cook at home. If you start off with good ingredients and good equipment, you really cannot go wrong.

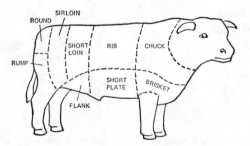

B E E F

Choice beef is the grade of beef most generally available in the supermarkets around the country. It is bright red in color, the cut bone ends are red, and the fat is white rather than cream-colored. It is coarser in texture than prime beef and the flavor will vary depending on the quality of the cattle, the method of feeding, and the age of the animal.

Prime beef is aged four to six weeks before it is sold. The carefully controlled aging process will result in an improved flavor and tenderness, but there will also be a considerable weight loss amounting to 10 per cent or more of its original bulk. As the beef is weighed before it is aged, it appears to cost more in weight comparison than choice beef. In fact the difference is not greatly significant because choice meat also loses weight from loss of moisture as it cooks.

Prime beef is darker in color than choice. It is also softer in texture and lightly marbled with thin rivulets of ivory-colored fat. A smaller piece of prime beef will be richer and more satisfying than a considerably larger piece of choice beef. Prime beef comes from the aristocracy of beef cattle, which are specially bred and fed for superior quality.

Every cut of beef provides the same food value in terms of protein, vitamins, and minerals, but just as some parts of the human body are more muscular than others, some cuts of meat are naturally more tender. The methods of cooking must be matched to the characteristics of the meat to obtain the best results.

CUT	METHOD OF COOKING
Filet steak	Pan-fry or broil
Porterhouse steak	Broil
Club steak	Broil
Strip steak	Broil
Sirloin steak	Broil
Minute steak	Pan-fry
Sirloin tip	Braise
Chuck steak	For stew and ground meat
Top and bottom round steak	For stew and ground meat
Flank steak	Marinate and broil
Short ribs	Boiled beef
Chuck roast	Pot roast
Shoulder roast	Pot roast
Brisket	Pot roast

Buy   ⅓ to ½ pound of boneless beef for each person, or ½ pound beef with a small bone such as sirloin steak. For each person allow ¾ pound of beef with a prominent bone such as standing rib or short ribs.

Storage   A 3- to 4-pound piece of beef for roasting will keep in the refrigerator for up to four days. Keep it loosely wrapped in the original paper so it can breathe or rewrap it if it is packed in plastic wrap. The beef must be able to breathe or it will deteriorate rapidly. Steak and stewing meat will keep for three days but ground beef and liver should be eaten as soon as possible and certainly within two days.

Beef can of course be frozen at zero degrees for up to six months. This is a considerably lower temperature than that at which ice cubes freeze, so if you are keeping beef in the freezer compartment of the refrigerator, check the exact temperature to be sure that the meat is safe. If the freezer is not maintained at zero degrees, do not keep it for longer than a month.

VEAL

The most tender veal is from milk-fed calves that are three months or younger. After this time the calves are fed on grain and allowed to graze. As their diet changes, the meat becomes pinker and pinker until in effect it is no longer veal, but baby beef. Because it is vastly more economical for farmers to fatten the cattle into mature animals, veal has become increasingly, almost prohibitively expensive meat.

When you are buying veal, look for white meat or very light pink meat with a firm texture. Avoid gray, watery-looking veal.

Buy ½ to ¾ pound boneless veal for two people, and allow two chops for each serving.

LAMB

The younger the lamb the more tender will be the meat. Baby lamb, the most expensive, is less than four months old, and lamb that is regularly for sale in the supermarket is about a year of age. The older the animal, the more pronounced the flavor becomes. The texture of meat from an older animal is coarser than that of a young lamb, and the fat tends to give it a somewhat gamy taste. Mutton makes good-tasting chops but is more frequently used for soups and stews rather than for roasts.

Buy 1 pound boneless lamb stew for two people and 2 pounds of lamb shanks for two people. Do not buy less than a 3-pound roast or it will become dry before it is fully cooked. When roasting any meats it is better to buy more than you need for one meal and use the leftovers another day. There are several recipes for leftovers in this book.

PORK

As with all meat, the younger it is the more moist and flavorful it will be. Always buy firm, fresh-looking pork. If it has been frozen and thawed in the supermarket, it will have a gray, limp appearance.

CHICKEN

You can tell the age and quality of a chicken just by looking at the way it is sitting. If it is plump with its skin fitting its body as if it were custom made, take it home. The breastbone will be red with bright blood. Beware the limp and jaundiced appearance of a skinny bird with flakes of ice beneath its back. It may have been frozen and defrosted more than once before being offered for your delight. A frying chicken can be fried, braised, stewed, or roasted, but a roasting chicken, which is an older bird, should only be roasted.

Buy   2½-pound chicken for two people. There will be some left over.

Storage   Wrap chicken in wax paper and cook it within three days.

⤐ MEAT TIMETABLE ⤏

Type	Oven Temperature	Time	
Beef			
Rib Roast	325°	Rare	15 min. per pound
4 pounds		Med.	18 min. per pound
		Well	22 min. per pound
Steak		Rare	7 min. per side
1″ thick	Broil	Med.	10 min. per side
		Well	18 min. per side
Hamburgers	Broil	Rare	5 min. per side
4 ounces		Med.	8 min. per side
		Well	10 min. per side

Stew 2½ pounds	350°		1½ hrs.
Flank steak	Marinate Broil		7 min. per side
Chicken			
2½ pounds	350°		50 min.
4 pounds	350°		80 min.
Parts	Broil		35 min.
Lamb			
4 pounds with bone	350°	Rare Med. Well	15 min. per pound 18 min. per pound 22 min. per pound
Without bone	350°		Add 10 min. per pound
Chops 1″ thick	Broil or fry	Rare Med. Well	8 min. per side 12 min. per side 15 min. per side
Veal			
Boned roast	350°		20 min. per pound
Scallopini	Fry		4 min. per side
Chops	Fry		7 min. per side
Ham			
Tenderized 6 to 12 pounds	350°		20 min. per pound
1″ slice	Fry or broil		10 min. per side
Pork			
Loin	350°		15 min. per pound
Chops	Fry or broil		10 min. per side
Spareribs	Marinate 350°		45 min.
Kidneys	Fry		10 min.
Liver slice	Fry		8 min. total cooking time

✄ BUYING VEGETABLES ✄

A vegetable will be at its peak of perfection when it has fully ripened in the sun. Ideally it should be eaten as close as possible to the time it has been harvested. If you can find asparagus in January grown in a faraway place, it will not only be considerably more costly than a local vegetable in season, but will neither taste as good nor have as high nutritional value. It is a sad fact that unless you grow your own vegetables or buy them from a local farm stand, commercially canned and frozen vegetables are less costly and have a greater food value than many supermarket "fresh" but underripe vegetables. Canned vegetables unfortunately lose both color and texture during processing, and much of the nutritional value lies in the liquid in which they are packed. For this reason, they should be reheated in their own liquid from the can. Frozen and canned vegetables are cooked briefly before being processed so need only to be reheated rather than actually cooked. Vitamins and minerals are destroyed by prolonged heat. Frozen and canned vegetables should be added to stews only during the last few minutes of the cooking period. Frozen vegetables should be reheated in as little water as possible.

Blanching and Parboiling   This is a method used for softening vegetables slightly before stuffing or adding to other short-cooking dishes. Carrots are partially cooked prior to glazing in butter; onions and green peppers are boiled for a few minutes before being threaded on skewers for shishkebabs. When the vegetables are prepared in advance, they should be plunged into a large pan of boiling salted water. Cook them uncovered over high heat until the water regains the boiling point. Boil for 2 minutes and drain in a colander. Rinse immediately under cold running water to stop the cooking. The vegetables will be crisp and bright in color. When you are ready to finish the cooking, return them to a pan of boiling water or toss them quickly in hot butter.

Steaming   To steam vegetables, pour an inch of water into a saucepan. Place the vegetables in a vegetable steamer, or a perforated plate or metal strainer, and suspend over the water. Cover and steam until tender but still retaining a slightly crisp texture.

Puréeing and Mashing   All manner of vegetables other than potatoes seem to have a completely different taste when they are mashed or puréed. The easiest way of puréeing is to put the vegetable, such as peas, cauliflower, spinach, or carrots into a blender. Add a tablespoon or two of butter and just enough cream or chicken broth to enable the blades to revolve easily. Taste and add more seasonings if necessary and return the vegetable to a buttered saucepan. Reheat until it is very hot. Puréed vegetables make an excellent accompaniment or may be served as a base for thinly sliced meats or boneless chicken breasts.

Braising Carrots, celery, leeks, white onions, and Belgian endives are particularly good when they are cooked in a liquid in the oven. Parboil the vegetable for 5 minutes to soften it slightly. Place in a buttered baking dish and add about ¼ inch of heavy cream, chicken or beef broth, a small onion, finely chopped, a pinch of salt, and a tablespoon of herbs. Cover the pan with aluminum foil and cook in a preheated 300° oven for 30–40 minutes until completely tender. The pan juices may then be thickened by adding 2 teaspoons of cornstarch, continue cooking for 5 minutes until the liquid has thickened into a sauce.

Baking Potatoes, acorn squash, and other varieties of winter squash are baked in the oven until they are tender. Potatoes are wrapped in foil and baked for at least 40 minutes. (It always seems to take 10 more minutes than you had anticipated.) Specific recipes for other baked and stuffed vegetables are included in the book.

Frying and Deep-Fat Frying Mushrooms, eggplant, cucumber, onions, and zucchini are some of the most frequently used vegetables for frying. They may be fried in oil, butter, or a combination of oil and butter. They can be cooked as they are or coated with egg and breadcrumbs. Deep-fried vegetables other than potatoes are usually dipped in batter and then cooked for 5 to 10 minutes.

⧭ BUYING AND PREPARING ⧭ VEGETABLES

Type	Season	Peak of Season
Artichokes	October–May	March and April

Buy 1 each

Choose fresh green color, closed, firm buds with little or no brown discoloration or ragged leaves. Discard lower outer leaves. Cut off stem so that the artichokes will stand without tipping on a plate. Plunge artichokes into a large saucepan of simmering water. Add 1 tablespoon vinegar or lemon juice and 2 teaspoons salt. Cover and simmer for 40 minutes or until a leaf can be pulled off easily. Drain and serve hot with melted butter or cold with vinaigrette sauce or mayonnaise-based sauce.

Asparagus   March–June   April and May
Buy 6 stalks for each person
Choose long, straight stalks of uniform size, tightly closed buds, and green almost the entire length of the stem. Wash carefully in a bowl of cold water to remove sand. Discard end or peel lower third with a potato peeler. Store wrapped in wet paper towels in the refrigerator. Tie in bundles and steam vertically in 2 inches of water for 10 minutes. A steamer can be improvised by inverting the inner part of a double boiler over the outer part.

String Beans   Year round   June–September
Buy ¾ pound for 2 people
Choose firm beans that snap briskly when broken rather than bend. Cut off ends and cut into desired length. Simmer uncovered for 10 minutes in salted water.

Beets   Year round   May–July
Buy 6 small beets for 2 servings
Choose firm small beets with fresh tops. Wash beets but do not peel or remove root. Cut leaves an inch from the beet. Place in a saucepan of boiling salted water. Cover and simmer for 20 minutes. Peel when cool enough to handle.

Broccoli   October–April   November–February
Generally available in 1½-pound bunches, which are sufficient for 3 people
Choose closed buds and firm, crisp stems. Wash in cold water. Discard lower third of stems. Cut stems lengthwise, dividing stem into four strips to speed cooking. Cover and simmer in salted water for 15 minutes. Test doneness with the point of a sharp knife.

Brussels Sprouts   September–February November and December
Available in 1-pound boxes sufficient for 3 servings
Select fresh, firm, small green buds free from brown or yellow leaves. Wash in cold water. Discard outer leaves. Cut a cross in the base at the stem end. Cover and simmer for 15 minutes in boiling salted water.

Cabbage   Year round   April and May
1 pound, the smallest size cabbage, will be sufficient for 4 servings
Choose green or red cabbage with loose rather than tightly closed head.

Cut into fourths and remove heavy stem. Discard outer leaves. Shred or cut into wedges and tie wedges with string in two places so the shape will be retained during cooking. Cover and simmer in salted water for 10 minutes.

Carrots   Year round   Year round
Allow 2 carrots for each serving
Choose fresh, straight, firm carrots with bright color. Store in a plastic bag in the refrigerator. Peel, cut into slices, sticks, or dice. Cover and simmer in salted water for 10–15 minutes depending on the size of the pieces. Test for doneness by tasting.

Celery   Year round   Year round
1 bunch makes 4 servings
Choose straight stems, do not buy brown or cracked stems. Store in a plastic bag. Save leaves for salads and soup. Cut into 2-inch lengths. Cover and simmer in salted water for 12 minutes or braise in the oven for 35 minutes.

Corn   May–August   June and July
Allow 1 or 2 ears for each serving
Choose corn with fresh and tightly closed outer leaves. Pull a leaf back and prick a kernel with a thumbnail to be sure it is moist and milky. Replace leaves and cook as soon as possible. Remove husks and cut off stem end. Place in boiling salted water. Cover and simmer for 4 minutes.

Eggplant   Year round   July and August
1 medium-sized eggplant is sufficient for 4 servings
Choose firm, well-rounded, uniform-colored eggplant free from blemishes and soft spots. Do not peel. Sprinkle slices with salt to draw out bitter juices. Leave to drain on a wire rack for 15 minutes. Pat dry on paper towels. Pan-fry in hot oil for 5 minutes on each side, or dip strips in batter and deep-fry for 8 minutes. Bake stuffed halves for 40 minutes.

Leeks   October–May   November–January
Allow 1 or 2 per person
Choose firm white bulb and fresh green tops. Do not buy dry-looking leeks. Discard root. Remove outer leaves. Divide top into long strips. Wash carefully to remove sand. Cut into slices for soups and stews or braise in the oven for 30 minutes.

Lettuce   Year round   Summer months
Store lettuce, unwashed, in plastic bags in the refrigerator. Cut or tear into bite-sized pieces and wash just before serving. Spin or pat leaves dry on paper towels.

Mushrooms   Year round   November–April
½ pound for 2 servings depending on specific recipe
Choose tightly closed pure white caps with moist stems. Discard ¼ inch at base of stem. Store in a plastic bag. Wipe with a damp cloth. Do not soak, as mushrooms absorb water. Slice, cut into quarters, or cook whole. Fry in hot butter for 3 minutes or sprinkle slices with lemon juice and serve raw in salads.

Okra   Year round   June–August
½ pound for 2 servings
Choose firm, small pods. Remove stem ends and wash carefully to remove sand. Cook small okra whole, cut large-sized okra into slices. Cover and simmer in salted water for 20 minutes.

White Onions   Year round   January–March
Buy 8 for 2 people
White onions are in theory milder than yellow onions, but this may not always be so. Peel onions and cut an x in each root end to prevent the inner core from falling out of the onion as it cooks.

Bermuda Onions   Year round   August
Buy 1 small onion for 2 people
Choose firm purple onion free from blemishes. Peel and slice very thinly for salads and cold dishes. Bermuda onions are too sweet to be used in cooking.

Peas   March–July   May and June
1½ pounds for 2 servings
Choose uniformly filled pods. Flat pods contain immature peas, and fat pods hold overripe peas. The pod should be juicy and firm. Shell peas. Cook uncovered in salted water with sprig of fresh mint and 1 teaspoon sugar added if desired. Boil for 5 minutes.

Peppers (Bell)   Year round   April–July
1 or 2 servings depending on recipe
Some varieties of peppers are green and others are red when fully ripe. Choose firm, brightly colored, well-shaped peppers. Remove stem, cut in half, and discard ribs and seeds. Chop into strips, circles, or dice.

Idaho Potatoes Year round June–August
Buy 1 per serving
Choose clean, firm potatoes of uniform size and free from blemishes and sprouts. Use for baking, French fries, boiled and mashed potatoes.

Long Island and
All-Purpose Potatoes Year round June–August
Use for potato salad, boiling, and mashing.

Sweet Potatoes September–March October to December
Choose uniformly sized potatoes with as few blemishes as possible. Do not buy sweet potatoes with soft spots or frost blemishes. Sweet potatoes may be baked, boiled, and mashed.

Scallions Year round August
Buy 1 bunch for 2 people
Choose thin, firm white bulbs with fresh green tops. Discard root but keep at least 1 inch of the green tops. Chop finely for use in salads, hot or cold dishes.

Shallots Year round November
Buy ½ pound (They keep in the refrigerator for at least a month.)
Buy firm shallots with light brown skin. Do not buy sprouting shallots or those that have soft spots. Use in salads and sauces.

Spinach Year round March–June
1 pound makes 3 servings
Choose fresh, brightly colored leaves. Discard heavy stems and soak in cold water for 5 minutes to remove sand. Lift spinach out of the water, rather than draining through a colander and pouring sandy water back over the leaves. Cook in a covered saucepan over low heat for 5 minutes using only the water clinging to the leaves, or, as recommended by the growers, fill a large pan with boiling salted water. Add the spinach. When the water regains boiling point, remove from the heat and leave to stand for 3 minutes. Drain.

Summer Squash
Zucchini Year round June–August
¾ pound squash for 2 people
Choose small, firm, yellow or green squash free from blemishes and soft spots. Wash and slice into ½-inch slices. Boil for 8 minutes or steam for 10–12 minutes. Allow 35 minutes for baked stuffed squash.

Winter Squash   September–February   September–December
1 large squash will be sufficient for 2 people
Choose firm, evenly colored squash. Cut in half and remove seeds. Add
butter, applesauce, and maple syrup or stuff with other ingredients. Cover
with aluminum foil and bake in a 350° oven for 45 minutes. May also
be peeled, cubed, and boiled for 30 minutes and mashed if desired.

Tomatoes   Year round   June–October
Buy plentifully in the summer   (Substitute canned tomatoes off season.)
Buy firm, unblemished tomatoes, bright red in color. Ideally then use immediately or, if necessary, store in the refrigerator and use as soon as possible.

⤳ STORING ⤶

Unpack groceries promptly.

If you have to keep frozen food in an emergency, wrap it in several layers
of newspaper.

Cut off extra leaves but do not prepare vegetables until ready to use.

Store lettuce, celery, and carrots in sealed plastic bags.

Keep watercress, leaves down, in a bowl of cold water in the refrigerator.

Wrap asparagus in wet tea towels or paper towels.

Keep potatoes, onions, and garlic in the refrigerator.

Keep bananas at room temperature.

Avocados, pears, pineapples, and melons continue to ripen at room temperature.

Store berries and other fruit on a flat tray. Do not wash until ready to
use.

Keep sliced bread, breadcrumbs, and coffee in the freezer.

Store opened packages of nuts in the refrigerator.

Transfer the contents of opened cans into covered glass jars or refrigerator
containers.

Store dried fruit in covered containers in the refrigerator.

Rewrap opened packages of luncheon meats and cheese in fresh transparent wrap each time the package is opened.

Store cookies in containers with tightly fitting lids. Do not combine crisp and soft cookies or sweet cookies and crackers.

Store eggs, small end down, in the refrigerator.

❧ HOW TO STOCK THE KITCHEN ❧

STAPLES

Tea bags
Coffee, regular and instant
Granulated sugar
Confectioners' sugar
Brown sugar
All-purpose flour
Baking soda
Baking powder
Cornstarch
Vegetable shortening
Vegetable oil
Salad oil
Olive oil
Vinegar
Baking chocolate
Sweet chocolate

Semisweet chocolate pieces
Spaghetti
Noodles
Rice
Hot cereal, dry cereal
Bouillon cubes
Unflavored gelatin
Salt
Cookies
Crackers
Pickles
Olives
Maple syrup
Jams, jellies and marmalade
Honey

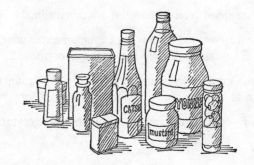

HERBS, SPICES, AND CONDIMENTS

Prepared mustard
Mayonnaise
Ketchup
Pickle relish
Chili sauce
Barbecue sauce
Worcestershire sauce
Steak sauce
Tabasco sauce
Vanilla extract
Almond extract

Cinnamon
Nutmeg
Paprika
Curry powder
Thyme
Bay leaves
Oregano
Rosemary
Basil
Dill
Tarragon

FRESH FOODS

Milk
Cream
Butter
Margarine
Eggs
Sour cream

Bacon
Sausage
Onions
Garlic
Carrots
Celery

Cheese
Ice cream
Meat
Fish
Poultry
Lunch meats
Frankfurters

Potatoes
Salad greens
Fresh vegetables
Fresh fruits
Lemons
Oranges

CANNED, BOTTLED, AND FROZEN FOODS

Soda
Tonic water
Club soda
Ginger ale
Beer

Fruit juices
Vegetables
Tomato sauce and paste
Tuna and salmon
Fruits

⤳ EQUIVALENCY TABLE ⤶

All-purpose flour	2 tablespoons	=	1 tablespoon cornstarch
Apples	1 pound	=	3 cups sliced
Baking chocolate	1 square	=	3 tablespoons regular cocoa and 2 teaspoons butter
Baking powder	1 teaspoon	=	¼ teaspoon baking soda and ½ teaspoon cream of tartar

Beans	1 pound dried	=	4 cups cooked
Bread	1 slice	=	½ cup crumbs
Butter	½ cup	=	8 tablespoons
Cake flour	1 cup	=	1 cup sifted all-purpose flour minus 2 tablespoons
Cheese	3 ounces cream	=	6 tablespoons
	¼ pound	=	1 cup grated
Egg	1 whole	=	2 egg yolks and 1 tablespoon water
Flour	1 pound	=	4 cups
Gelatin	1 package	=	1 tablespoon
Graham crackers	15 sections	=	1 cup crumbs
Herbs	1 teaspoon dried	=	1 tablespoon fresh
Lemon	1 whole	=	3 tablespoons juice
	Rind 1 whole	=	1 tablespoon grated
Nuts	5⅓-ounce can	=	1 cup whole
	4½-ounce package	=	1 cup chopped
Orange	1 whole	=	½ cup juice
	Rind 1 whole	=	2 tablespoons grated
Rice	1 cup raw	=	3 cups cooked
Sugar	1 pound granulated	=	2½ cups
	1 pound powdered	=	4 cups
Tomatoes	1 pound	=	3 medium sized

⚘ AN HERB AND SPICE CHART ⚘

Allspice	Pickling Pumpkin pie Apple pie Fruitcakes
Basil	All tomato dishes Broiled fish Shrimp Liver
Bay leaves	Poached fish Pot roast Stews Marinades
Cardamon	Ham Pork Hot mulled wine Breads Cakes
Chili	Ground beef Barbecue sauce Beans
Cinnamon	Fruits Custards Coffee Chicken Tea
Cloves	Marinades Apple pie Beef stew Spice cakes

Dillweed	Cheese dishes Salads Fish Pickles
Ginger	Melon Pork Pot roast Gingerbread
Marjoram	Pâté Stewed meats Broiled fish Spaghetti sauce
Mustard powder	Mayonnaise Chicken Eggs Pork
Nutmeg	Scrambled eggs Pies Hot drinks Cakes Puddings
Oregano	Tomatoes Spaghetti and other pasta dishes Fish
Paprika	Canapés Egg dishes Beef stew Cheese dishes Batters
Rosemary	Lamb Tomato sauce
Saffron	Shellfish Cakes Rice
Sage	Chicken Dried beans Pork Tea

Savory	Vegetables
	Soup
	Eggs
	Chicken
Tarragon	Fish
	Chicken
	Eggs
	Sauces
Thyme	Soups
	All meats
	Eggs
	Stews
Turmeric	Canning
	Curried eggs

EATING – A WEIGHTY SUBJECT

Many people have a very funny attitude toward food. We eat at least three times a day and still look forward to the next meal as though it will be an entirely new experience. If we survive the day without breakfast or lunch, we feel it necessary to inform anybody who will listen that we have performed this extraordinary sacrifice. If we missed a meal because we were working, the work itself acquires a dignity bordering on mystical achievement. We seek sympathetic approval for having fasted even if we went without lunch involuntarily or because we simply forgot to eat. After eight hours without food we are reduced to a state of near desperation. Even a terrible greasy hamburger, which will arrive quickly, is a more appealing prospect than a lobster soufflé.

Good food is not necessarily rich or elaborate food. In fact, the better the quality of the ingredients, the simpler the preparation can be. But on the other hand, there are all manner of foods that, though they do not cause demonstrable gastronomic eruptions, can be bad for you.

A hamburger contains roughly four hundred fifty calories, most of which are beginning to race around your body looking for a permanent resting place before you have gone fifteen blocks from the neon sign. It is not that the hamburger is necessarily bad; it is just that it is usually not good. There are exceptions, of course. The main trouble with a hamburger is that it is just a hamburger and there are so depressingly many of them. They no longer create any excitement. There is no mystery about a hamburger. You know in advance how it is going to taste, so, feeling marginally, subliminally disappointed, you go on opening and closing the refrigerator door all evening looking for a little something to satisfy an indefinable craving for deliciousness, even when you are not really hungry.

Everybody knows the difference between good food and food. Give even a child who has a constant diet of cornflakes, French fries, and potato chips a chunk of homemade bread hot from the oven. Spread it with creamy butter and homemade strawberry preserves. Let him sit on the kitchen floor and ruminate over it and he will know it is good. He will remember it as he remembers the apple that ripened on the tree just so he could steal it. He does not need to be told that the stolen apple tasted infinitely better than the one in the shrink-wrapped package on the green cardboard tray in the brown bag from the supermarket. His satisfaction is not entirely related to his natural criminal instincts either. . . .

Good food is good and small quantities of it are more satisfying than larger quantities of food that doesn't look, smell, or taste good. If you are not satisfied with the food aesthetically, you tend to eat too much and make a whole new set of problems for yourself. If constant weight is to be maintained, it is necessary to balance the intake and output of calories. It may therefore not be entirely wise to eat the very last spoonful of a hot fudge sundae, merely to satisfy an absent mother who always insisted that you eat everything on your plate. The body needs approximately fifteen calories a day for each pound of weight. In other words, the average woman (there is no such thing) who weighs one hundred and twenty pounds needs roughly eighteen hundred calories a day so that she neither gains nor loses weight. This is very approximate, as other factors such as her height, age, and amount of activity must also be taken into account. A man needs roughly two hundred calories a day more than a woman. This figure assumes the man is not lounging around watching daytime television while his fair young bride is rushing home from a busy day at the office laden with groceries and contemplating whether to make the dinner, do the laundry, or wash the kitchen floor before she spends the evening playing squash. Most figures can be juggled to fit the circumstances.

It may be possible to prove conclusively that, if you dine only on exquisitely dainty morsels, you will have no problem with excess weight, but as a practical matter many people do not eat sensibly, so they are forced to think occasionally, though not to the point of preoccupation, about calories. For those who soothe their anxieties by indulging themselves in mini food orgies, a few passing thoughts may be worth considering. . . .

More than one out of four people are overweight. A condition that has numerous disadvantages but not a single advantage.

Being overweight does not make anybody happy, nor is it good for you. It is bad for your heart and your circulatory system. It increases the risks of high blood pressure and enables insurance companies to charge you higher premiums for life insurance. Some employers will not hire you and some clothing manufacturers will ignore you or charge you for every inch of fabric they deem necessary to clothe you modestly. But even without these tangibly terrible things happening, you just feel unbeautiful, uncomfortable, self-conscious, and unhappy. If you eat because your unhappiness overwhelms you, you become like the snake who swallows his own tail.

It is extremely difficult to get fat except by eating. In spite of the claims some make and half believe, there is no possible way (unless you have hypothyroidism) that you can expand your waistline by merely glancing in the direction of a cream-filled doughnut. It is when you reach for it, open your mouth, pop it in that the trouble starts. If you turn away from temptation and eat just a little less at each meal, you will lose weight, though not perhaps as quickly as you would like.

It takes 3,500 calories to produce a pound of fat. In order to lose that pound in one week, you must reduce your intake of calories by five hundred every day. If you reduce your intake of calories more drastically, you will of course lose more weight, but the side effects of depression, irritability, and lethargy dictate that it is better for you and those who live with you to be rational about your level of expectations concerning weight loss. After all, it took a certain amount of effort to accumulate the extra pounds, so set a realistic goal to remove them again. Learn the number of calories in the foods you eat regularly and force yourself to stay away from at least some foods that are notoriously fattening. Tell yourself you are bored with eating peanuts at every cocktail party. They always taste the same anyway. Eventually you may be able to believe yourself and become a connoisseur of carrot sticks. Remember too, even if you eat in bed in the dark, the calories are still being counted and deposited somewhere.

Steam baths and sweaty, violent exercises result in a minor loss of weight. However, the body tends to become greatly dehydrated at the same time. Have a beer as a reward for winning three straight sets of tennis in ninety-eight-degree heat and you would have been thinner if you had lain on the beach and read a good book.

Crash diets can be actually harmful to your health unless supervised by a reputable doctor. Liquid diets make you yearn so desperately for a solid meal you may end up eating more than your normal quantity of food. Worry earnestly about the psychological and therapeutic value of eating seaweed, tree bark, and dietetic dog biscuits before you commit yourself to them as a way of life. If you come to the unshakable belief

that you have such a serious lack of will power that you honestly prefer
to spend exorbitant sums of money on such things rather than making do
with a simple poached trout and fresh cucumber salad nestled cozily on
a dewy fresh leaf of Boston lettuce, you are really missing a lot. There
is such a variety of glorious foods that contain very few calories it seems
a pity to throw away your money on questionable alternatives.

THE DINNER HOUR

Almost everybody remembers one or two truly remarkable meals,
though efforts to re-create them are predictably doomed to failure, for it
is not only the food but the nostalgia of the moment that cannot be brought
back. It is the company, the mood, the place, the intangibles, felt more
than acknowledged, that made the memory so retrospectively entrancing.
The food was merely the focus of the event. You may in fact have eaten
far better meals under different circumstances, wiped your mouth on a
snowy white napkin, and simply walked away without a comment. I only
mention this because it is sometimes disheartening to spend a great deal
of time and effort to produce a poundcake or spaghetti sauce just like
somebody's mother's only to be told something is missing. It is the emotion
that is missing, your spaghetti sauce may be sublime.

Food is inextricably entwined with our broad heritage and personal
experiences. We feel guilty about throwing away even scraps of anything
edible, though we would not hesitate to lay aside another project that no
longer captured our interest. We read so much about the starving millions
of the world, yet, as deep and compassionate as our sympathies are, re-
alistically it does not help them if we eat a rotten tomato or add it to
the soup pot in the vain hope that when it is submerged in boiling broth
and heated it will bring forth a magnificent flavor from its departed soul.
If something has gone irretrievably or even marginally bad, it does not
help to wring your hands, though a few good resolutions may be appropriate to the occasion.

Unlike almost anything else, food is bound up with love. Reject my
food and you reject me. Eat and you love me. Eat two helpings and you
love me more. Eat and eat and eat and eat and you become uncomfortable,
bad tempered, unbeautiful, and unwell and then what? Little has been
gained except excess weight. On the other hand, even a legally constituted
lover is only rarely permitted, and then under totally idyllic circumstances,
to comment that there is too much salt in the soup. You know, of course,
as well as he that there is, so rather than getting angry at the criticism

(which suggests hitherto unrevealed traits of male chauvinism, lack of understanding, insensitivity, and unrequited love) simply agree. At times of crisis like this do not feel tempted to suggest that he make the dinner himself, unless you really mean it, or to declare either hotly or tearfully that he leave the table permanently. It might, however, not be a bad idea to add a little less salt next time.

If anybody tucks his napkin under his chin and dives cheerfully into a breath-takingly exotic dessert brimming with cream and butter and all manner of other deliciousnesses, moaning all the time about the calories he is quite voluntarily consuming, offer, graciously, never to make such a thing again. For the sake of emphasis you could go on to swear you will only make broiled fish and raw carrots in the future. That should stop the flow of remarks abruptly. It seems to some that the discussion of calories while in the act of consuming them is an outrage even though the verbal wallowing in the ecstasy of guilt may be intended as a compliment to the cook.

Nothing is more depressing or guaranteed to halt all further culinary efforts than toiling for hours, cheerfully, willingly, even enthusiastically, in the kitchen making a baba drenched with rum and floating among a thousand rosettes of whipped cream only to be greeted with "I do not think I will have dessert, thank you." Nor does it inspire anyone to produce a paella consisting of scarlet lobsters, shrimp, mussels, chicken, sausages, and bright green peas all nestled snugly in a bed of steaming golden rice when all the while you know the other person would prefer a steak and an aluminum potato. Unless it is already too late, it is wise to regard anyone who will eat only what he had eaten before with extreme suspicion and utmost caution. It is infinitely more rewarding to choose a man of adventurous tastes as a lifelong dining companion.

Then there is the question of the guests. What do you do with those helpful people who keep trotting out to the kitchen to see how you are getting along? Do you tell them politely but firmly that you want to be alone, if that is the way you feel, or do you say you will call them if you need them and then don't call? Then they, conscience pangs allayed, can return to the other guests. The alternative is to invite them in, and everybody else if you like, depending on the people and the formality of the dinner. This is sometimes a cheerful and relaxing way of getting the dinner together and works well as long as everybody has a drink and an inch or two of counter to lean against.

I personally find it disturbing or, to put it more honestly, intensely annoying to have guests jumping up and down between courses bearing forth dirty dishes, or even worse, appallingly worse, start clattering around in the privacy of the dishwasher, stacking plates, talking gaily while I am in a calm frenzy trying to figure out how to scrounge up eight more matching plates and at the same time float serenely into the dining room, where

I will present a breath-taking creation, step back, and, with charming modesty and feigned deprecating little smiles, accept the applause of the assembled multitude. It is an impossibility to perform this ridiculous charade with Milly running the water in the kitchen sink and leaping about in the background. If you happen to feel as neurotic about this as I, banish her from your guest list forever or, if you must, invite her for hot dogs and paper plates.

The foregoing has assumed that all was swimming along perfectly at the command center and you are still the captain of the ship. But what to do, alas, if everything is beginning to fall apart or, worse, has already gone irretrievably wrong? The sensible thing to do is to laugh. This, of course, is absolutely not possible. The first thing to do then is to go and comb your hair, even if it does not need it. Then walk back calmly to the kitchen and try and take stock of the situation as rationally as possible. (Cooking is often not so much the art of creation as the art of retrieval.) If the sauce has curdled, try and pull it back together again by beating some of the curdled sauce into a fresh egg yolk. If that does not work— and, given the emotion of the situation, it may well not—simply make the decision not to serve it at all. In either case do not, under any circumstances, mention it. If anybody else comments on the fact that they saw a sauce in the kitchen, assume a firm though glazed expression and change the subject with as much skill as you can muster on such brief notice.

If the roast is undercooked, carve it from one end and then, again without comment, slice it authoratively from the other end as though this was the normal practice in your household. The ends will be more done than the center. Then with all due undetectable haste put it back in the oven, at furnace temperature, and serve it fifteen minutes later as an encore.

If the roast is overdone, there is absolutely nothing you can do or say to remedy the situation. So do not spend any time drawing attention to it. The guests, if cheerful enough, or discreet enough, are not likely to say what a terrible piece of overdone beef this is. Tragedies happen to even the best and most experienced of cooks at times, and a solid friendship can withstand a little overdone meat. A small glass of brandy after a nerve-racking dinner may stem the flow of tears while two small glasses of brandy will enable you to devise a way of throwing the entire blame on someone else.

Finally it is all over—except the dishes. The puritan ethic demands that they be dispatched forthwith. Mothers and particularly mothers-in-law always wash dishes before going to bed. At the end of the evening you may feel, though, that you would just like to go to bed in your present mood and leave everything where it is. Follow your inclination, there will be time enough the next day for you to feel sorry you did.

⌇ MENU PLANNING ⌇

Almost all recipes can be prepared in two or more stages with hours or even days between the completion of one step and the next. It is particularly important to pace the cooking for a dinner party so you do not feel exhausted or harassed when the guests arrive.

Work out the menu carefully to eliminate as many last-minute steps as possible. If you are having a meat or fish that requires very close attention to the timing, do not serve an artichoke for the appetizer. An artichoke takes such a deliciously long time to eat that you will find yourself jumping up and down from the table to check on the next course while all the guests are still eating the first course. It is better to eliminate the first course entirely; serve it in another room before you start cooking the meat or have a simple hors d'oeuvre that can be savored and whisked away after it has set the stage for the entree.

It is a great help to arrange the meal so that two of the three courses are completely prepared in advance and are ready for serving without any last-minute touches. For example, have soup and a cold dessert with a more elaborate main course, or have a hot appetizer and a cold entree.

If soufflés are a specialty of the house, it is less worrying and equally spectacular to serve the soufflé for an appetizer rather than dessert. However, if you have your heart set on a sweet soufflé, prepare the base in advance and leave it at room temperature. Beat the egg whites thirty minutes before you plan to serve it, fold the whites into the base, and transfer the ingredients to the prepared dish. The progress of the meal can be extended and made more flexible by serving the salad and cheese after the entree in the traditional French manner, and will make the timing of the soufflé less critical. Nothing is impossible, but some things do tend to make the flow of the meal a little more tricky and require a higher degree of concentration.

I think it is important to keep the food reasonably simple. It is not entirely necessary to dazzle the guests with your culinary virtuosity with each dish. It is, after all, a triumph to be able to cook the asparagus, carrots, or boiled potatoes to the exact point of perfection without having to complicate everything to the point of absurdity with sauces, cheese toppings, slivered almonds and goodness knows what else. In this context restrain yourself from serving more than one complex sauce with the dinner. If the meat is served in a sauce, or if you are making a stew, do not fabricate a complicated or sauced vegetable accompaniment dish but keep the other foods in their purest natural state.

It goes without saying that rich, soft, creamy food should not be followed by more rich, creamy food or it becomes like eating butter without bread. No matter how good each individual dish may be, the total effect is lost in a blur of sameness.

Chinese cooking at its best works on the principle of yin and yang, dominant and recessive, and this theory works equally well applied to all cooking. Each ingredient must have a reason for its inclusion, or it must not be there at all. Spicy food is balanced with bland (curry in India is served with yoghurt, a French pepper steak is prepared with a cream-enriched Madeira sauce, and fish is served with the contrasting sharpness of lemon). Every firm texture needs a balancing softness to enhance the characteristics of each, and color contrasts are assembled in harmony because we eat first with our eyes.

Compare, in your mind's eye, a plate of mashed potatoes, poached chicken breasts with cream sauce, and cauliflower with the much better idea of serving saffron rice, roast chicken with tomato sauce, and string beans. These are all extremely simple foods, simply prepared, and though the example is slightly ridiculous, it is surprising how often even experienced cooks commit similar errors using more sophisticated dishes in more intricate arrangements.

Keep the food appropriate to the occasion. This suggestion may also seem entirely superfluous, but it is easy to get carried away with the enthusiasm of making something extra special. Racking your brains for an idea, you come up with the notion of taking a quiche to share with friends at a football game. You know the people. You know they like quiche, but it is never as good as when it is just made; it is difficult to carry, awkward to serve, and impossible to eat in one hand with gloves on! If you think these potential problems all the way through, you may decide to take something else along. Individual thermos flasks of hot, hot minestrone or thick pea soup would be a great comfort on a cold winter afternoon, and though they are a little heavy, flasks are easily carried in a shopping bag. By the same reasoning, little piping hot hors d'oeuvres are delectable seated at a table, but when they are passed on a tray at a crowded cocktail party they must be firm in texture, for few things taste so good that they are worth the risk of spilling down a Lanvin tie or its equivalent.

After a movie, have the ingredients ready so everybody can prepare their own sandwiches or make something that is very easy and does not require a long wait or undue fussing. Save the flaming baked Alaska for a leisurely evening at home. Ultimately cooking and entertaining should be a pleasure, not a burden, so keep a sense of balance and it will make life much easier.

CANDLELIGHT DINNERS FOR TWO

⚹ MENU SUGGESTIONS ⚹

Shrimp with Garlic
Roast Cornish Hens with Vegetables
Caramelized Pineapple

◆

Cream of Lettuce Soup
Pepper Steak
Strawberries Romanoff

◆

Pears with Prosciutto
Chicken Kiev
Crepes Suzettes

◆

Mediterranean Mussels
Veal with Lemon and Brandy
Cherries Jubilee

◆

Onion Soup
Sirloin Steak with Wine Sauce
Grand Marnier Soufflé

◆

Chicken and Ham in Fresh Peaches
Poached Salmon
Hollandaise Sauce
Homemade Ice Cream

⚥ CANDLELIGHT DINNERS FOR TWO ⚥

A candlelight dinner is the setting for the happiest of all evenings. There are few occasions to rival the sharing of a good meal with the one person you have chosen to be with at this moment. It is a time to fill with all the self-indulgent pleasures of wining and dining, of giving and receiving. Acres of uninterrupted deliciousness.

There is a particular joy in creating this atmosphere, for it is made up of many parts, each dependent on the other, and everything that heightens the joy is appropriate to the event. The food and wine will be selected with infinite care, the table set with all the finest of fineries; flowers and candles, mood and music, and everything will be in readiness for a slow, measured smooth succession of glorious things to eat and drink.

A candlelight dinner can also be a candle in an empty jam jar, plastic plates, and no chairs to sit on, and still be memorable, marvelous in fact. But even under these circumstances, the food is still of supreme importance. If you serve a carry-out meal from your local Charlie Wang's chopstick emporium, it will not be a candlelight dinner even though the candles are alight.

The recipes follow. Remember to blow out the candles as you tiptoe away.

SALAD OF SHRIMP AND ARTICHOKE BOTTOMS

Throughout this book I have attempted to steer away from French terminology as much as possible. This does not, in any way suggest anti-Gallic feeling, quite to the contrary, but I do think that terms such as "sauté" tend to be a little elitist when compared with a readily available word like "fry." However, fonds d'artichauts *has a certain cachet that is missing when the words become translated to artichoke bottoms. If you are serving this dish by candlelight, you might feel happier to make a total commitment and call it* une salade de crevettes avec fonds d'artichauts!

FOR 2

2 canned or fresh artichoke bottoms

DRESSING

¼ teaspoon salt

Freshly ground black pepper

¼ teaspoon tarragon

1 tablespoon lemon juice

3 tablespoons oil

¼ pound tiny shrimp

1 small tomato, peeled, seeded,
   and chopped

1 hard-cooked egg, chopped

Place the artichoke bottoms on serving plates.

Combine the ingredients for the dressing and toss with the shrimp, tomato, and egg. Drain and pile on top of the artichoke bottoms.

COMMENT: Many variations can be made on this theme. The shrimp, egg, and tomato may be combined with mayonnaise flavored with mustard or with chopped chutney and placed on top of the artichoke bottoms.

POTTED SHRIMP

A cocktail or sandwich spread.

½ pound tiny fresh, raw shrimp,
   peeled

½ pound butter

⅛ teaspoon mace

⅛ teaspoon allspice

1 teaspoon paprika

¼ teaspoon salt

Freshly ground black pepper

2 tablespoons lemon juice

If you are using small shrimp as opposed to the really tiny Danish shrimp, cut them into very small pieces.

Melt the butter and strain it through several layers of cheesecloth to form clarified butter. Do not squeeze the cloth to obtain the last few drops of butter, even though it seems outrageously expensive not to do so. Pour 3 tablespoons of the clarified butter into a small frying pan. Heat until hot. Add the shrimp and spices and cook over high heat for 2 minutes. Remove from the heat and add the lemon juice.

Place the shrimp in a small pot or crock, pressing them down lightly. Spoon the remaining clarified butter over the shrimp to seal the pot.

COMMENT: The butter is clarified to remove the solid part. In this form the butter will keep for a considerably longer period and preserve the shrimp. Clarified butter can be heated to a very high temperature before it burns.

SHRIMP WITH GARLIC

The preparation and cooking time for this appetizer is less than 15 minutes.   FOR 2

¾ pound large shrimp
 2 tablespoons butter
 4 scallions, finely chopped
 2 cloves garlic, finely chopped
 1 teaspoon paprika
¼ teaspoon oregano
 2 teaspoons lemon juice
 1 tablespoon white vermouth
 6 cherry tomatoes, cut in half and
      seeds removed
 2 tablespoons finely chopped parsley
Crusty bread

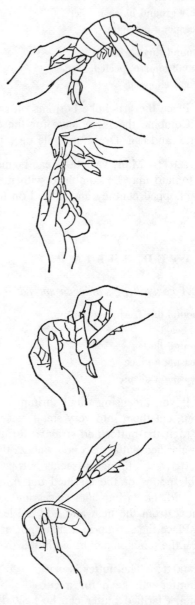

Peel the shrimp. Cut the shrimp in half lengthwise and open the halves so that each shrimp lies flat.

Heat the butter in a frying pan. Add the scallions and garlic and fry for 3 minutes. Add the shrimp and cook, stirring constantly, for 3 minutes until pink. Add all the remaining ingredients except crusty bread and continue cooking for 3 or 4 minutes.

Serve immediately with crusty bread.

COMMENT: There is far greater danger of overcooking than of undercooking the shrimp, so keep a sharp eye on the timing.

SHRIMP COCKTAIL SAUCE

Almost everything made freshly at home tastes better than anything made in a factory.   FOR 1 POUND SHRIMP

1 cup tomato ketchup	2 teaspoons lemon juice
1 teaspoon prepared horseradish	1 clove garlic, minced
Dash cayenne pepper	½ teaspoon chili powder

Combine all the ingredients.

COMMENT: The shrimp will have more flavor if they are not served icy cold.

MEDITERRANEAN MUSSELS

The mussels can be served as a "soup" or with rice as a main course. Dip crusty bread into the sauce.   FOR 2

2 dozen fresh mussels	2 tablespoons finely chopped
1 cup white wine	parsley
2 tablespoons olive oil	1 tablespoon fresh basil
1 onion, finely chopped	or ½ teaspoon dried basil
1 clove garlic, finely chopped	½ teaspoon salt
1 green pepper, finely chopped	Freshly ground black pepper
2 small tomatoes, peeled, seeded, and chopped	

Scrub the mussels and remove the "beards." Pour the wine into a saucepan. Add the mussels. Cover and steam the mussels over low heat in 1" simmering water for 5 minutes until they have opened. Discard the empty half shells and strain the liquid through several layers of cheesecloth.

Heat the oil and fry the onion, garlic, and green pepper for 5 minutes. Add the strained liquid and all the remaining ingredients except the mussels. Simmer uncovered for 15 minutes until the liquid has reduced slightly.

Add the mussels in the remaining half shells, and simmer for 3 more minutes until the mussels are hot. Ladle into soup bowls.

COMMENT: If the recipe is prepared in advance, add the cooked mussels when the soup is reheated.

ANCHOVIES WITH PIMIENTOS

An inspired combination to eat before a bowl of spaghetti.   FOR 2

4 leaves Boston lettuce	1 tablespoon oil
2-ounce can anchovy fillets	2 scallions, finely chopped
2-ounce jar pimientos, drained	1 hard-cooked egg, finely chopped
1 teaspoon vinegar	1 tablespoon finely chopped parsley

Line 2 plates with lettuce leaves. Arrange anchovy fillets like the spokes of a wheel from the center to the edges of the plates. Arrange pimientos in similar fashion between the anchovies. Stir the vinegar and oil together and sprinkle over the salad. Place the scallions in the centers of the plates. Garnish with egg and parsley.

COMMENT: If you find that the flavor of anchovies is too strong, soak them in milk for 15 minutes. Rinse under cold running water and pat dry on paper towels. Give the milk to a friendly cat.

PEARS WITH PROSCIUTTO

A quick and elegant first course.   FOR 2

1 large, luscious, juicy pear, peeled, cored, and halved	6 slices prosciutto ham
Boston lettuce leaves	Freshly ground black pepper

TARRAGON CREAM DRESSING

¼ cup mayonnaise   ½ teaspoon sugar
1 teaspoon tarragon vinegar

Place the pear halves on plates lined with lettuce leaves. Arrange ham over the pears and dust with pepper.

Mix the ingredients for the dressing and serve immediately.

COMMENT: The tarragon cream dressing is also good served with cold cooked asparagus or green beans.

CHICKEN AND HAM IN FRESH PEACHES

This unusual first course is a variation on the classic theme of melon and prosciutto ham. If you do not happen to have these particular ingredients, use leftover pork or ham and fold them into the flavored mayonnaise.

FOR 2

2 medium-sized fresh peaches
Boston lettuce leaves
4 slices prosciutto ham, sliced
    paper thin
1 whole chicken breast, poached in
    ½ cup chicken broth for
    8 minutes

½ cup mayonnaise
1 tablespoon dry sherry
1 teaspoon prepared Dijon mustard
2 teaspoons fresh dill or finely
    chopped parsley

Plunge the peaches into boiling water for 10 seconds and then into cold water. Remove the skins. Cut each peach in half and place cavity side up on plates lined with Boston lettuce leaves.

Chop the ham and chicken into dice. Combine the mayonnaise, sherry, mustard, and dill or parsley. Fold the ham and chicken into the mayonnaise and fill the peach cavities with this mixture.

ARTICHOKE HEARTS WITH DILL SAUCE

An easily prepared appetizer. The dill sauce can also be used for sliced tomatoes and barely cooked string beans or asparagus tips. FOR 2

8-ounce jar artichoke hearts
½ teaspoon salt
Freshly ground black pepper
2 tablespoons lemon juice

8 tablespoons olive oil
4 tablespoons fresh dillweed
    or 1 teaspoon dried dill
Shredded Boston lettuce

Drain the artichoke hearts.

Place all the remaining ingredients in the empty jar and shake vigorously. Return the artichokes to the jar and leave to marinate for at least an hour. Invert the jar from time to time. Serve on a bed of shredded Boston lettuce.

COMMENT: When the artichokes have been eaten, replace them with small mushroom caps or another vegetable and you will have a quick appetizer always on hand.

ONION SOUP

A bowl of onion soup may be the beginning of the ending of a cold winter night.   FOR 2

Preheat the oven to 250°.

1 tablespoon oil	2 tablespoons apple brandy
1 tablespoon butter	(optional)
2 small onions, thinly sliced	¼ cup grated Swiss or Gruyère
2 teaspoons flour	cheese
2½ cups beef broth	1 tablespoon grated Parmesan
2 slices French bread	cheese

Heat the oil and butter in a saucepan. Add the onions and stir over low heat for 5 minutes until softened. Stir in the flour and add the beef broth. Cover and simmer for 20 minutes.

In the meantime, toast the bread on a cookie sheet in a 250° oven for 20 minutes until it is completely dry and crisp.

Add the apple brandy to the soup and ladle into 2 bowls. Top with bread and combined cheeses. Place under the broiler for 4 minutes until the cheese has melted and is bubbling and lightly browned.

COMMENT: If the bowls will not fit under the broiler, place the bread and cheese in the bowls before adding the soup. The heat of the soup will melt the cheese.

CREAM OF LETTUCE SOUP

What an odd idea, you may think, but in the summer when the lettuce is plentiful and inexpensive, this is a lovely, delicate opening course.

FOR 2

1 tablespoon butter	1 teaspoon curry powder
4 scallions, finely chopped	½ cup peeled, cored, and thinly
2 tablespoons white vermouth	sliced apples
3 cups shredded leaf, Bibb, or Boston	2 cups chicken broth
lettuce	2 tablespoons sour cream

Melt the butter in a saucepan. Add all the remaining ingredients except the chicken broth and sour cream. Cover and simmer over very low heat for 15 minutes. Add the chicken broth and simmer for 10 more minutes. Purée the soup in a blender and serve hot or cold topped with sour cream.

COMMENT: The term "sweating" is used to describe vegetables cooked in a small quantity of liquid. This process brings out all the flavor while retaining the color and texture of the vegetable.

GAZPACHO

A delectable soup for the summer when all the ingredients are at the peak of ripeness.

FOR 2

2 small tomatoes, peeled, seeded, and chopped	¼ teaspoon salt
4 scallions, finely chopped	Freshly ground black pepper
1 clove garlic, finely chopped	1 tablespoon lemon juice
½ green pepper, finely chopped	4 tablespoons oil
½ cup cucumber, seeds removed and diced	¾ cup chicken broth, chilled
	2 tablespoons finely chopped parsley (optional)

Place the tomatoes, scallions, garlic, pepper, and cucumber in a bowl, preferably a glass bowl, so that all the colors will show to full effect. Combine the salt, pepper, lemon juice and oil and pour over the vegetables. Leave to marinate from an hour or longer if possible. Just before serving add the cold chicken broth and sprinkle with parsley.

COMMENT: Though these are the traditional ingredients for making gazpacho, other raw fresh vegetables may also be added to the soup.

AVOCADO SOUP

A silken soup that can be made in less than 5 minutes.   FOR 2

1 ripe avocado
1¼ cups cold chicken broth
½ cup sour cream
½ cup light cream or milk
2 teaspoons lemon juice

½ teaspoon salt
Grated rind of 1 lemon
1 tablespoon chopped chives
Freshly grated black pepper

Peel the avocado, cut it into slices, and place in the blender with the chicken broth, sour cream, light cream, lemon juice, and salt. Blend until smooth and pour into individual soup bowls. Garnish with lemon rind and chopped chives and sprinkle with black pepper.

COMMENT: If you decide to make the soup in advance, place the avocado pit in the bowl and it will prevent the soup from darkening.

STEAK FLAMING IN BRANDY

This recipe can be prepared with sirloin steak but is even better with filet.   FOR 2

2 filet steaks, 1½" thick
2 tablespoons butter

1 tablespoon oil

TOPPING

2 tablespoons butter
4 scallions, finely chopped
4 mushrooms, finely chopped
1 tablespoon chopped chives

1 tablespoon finely chopped parsley
2 teaspoons Worcestershire sauce
Freshly ground black pepper
2 tablespoons brandy

Trim the filet steaks and fry over high heat for 5 minutes on each side in combined hot butter and oil.

In the meantime, heat the remaining 2 tablespoons of butter in a small frying pan. Add the scallions and mushrooms and fry over moderate heat for 5 minutes. Stir in the chives, parsley, Worcestershire sauce and season with pepper. Transfer the steaks to a hot serving plate and top with the scallion mixture.

Heat the brandy in a small pan. Do not let it get too hot or it will ignite spontaneously. Bring the steaks to the table. Light the warm brandy with a match and pour the flames over the steaks.

Note: The steaks may also be flamed directly in the pan. Add the brandy and light it with a match.

COMMENT: There are few things that make you feel more foolish than attempting to make a major production out of something that ultimately does not work. When you heat the brandy first and then light it in the pot, it is guaranteed to flame. If you shake the plate to scatter the flames, the brandy will become diluted with the meat juices and the flames will be extinguished immediately, leaving behind a puddle of alcohol. The idea of flaming is to create an essence of brandy and burn off the alcohol.

STEAK TARTARE

If all things were possible in the best of all possible worlds, the steak should be ground at home immediately before it is eaten. Ground beef darkens every minute that it is exposed to the air, and if you are going to eat raw steak, it must be made with fresh, fresh, fresh-looking beef.

FOR 2

¾–1 pound tenderloin or round steak, ground twice
½ cup finely chopped shallots or scallions
¾ teaspoon salt

Freshly ground black pepper
2 eggs, separated
¼ cup red wine
4 anchovy fillets
2 teaspoons capers

Place the beef, shallots or scallions, salt, pepper, egg whites, and wine in a bowl. Mix the ingredients and form into 2 patties. Make a depression in the top of each patty and fill each with an unbroken egg yolk. Cut anchovy fillets in half lengthwise and arrange in a crisscross pattern over the patties. Garnish with capers.

Serve immediately with freshly made toast and a small salad of Boston lettuce and cherry tomatoes dressed with oil and vinegar.

COMMENT: If you would like to talk yourself into buying a meat grinder, it is a very practical utensil to aid in using leftover meats.

PEPPER STEAK

The filet is the tenderest of all steaks, and perhaps this is one of the very best ways of cooking it.   FOR 2

2 filet steaks cut 1″ thick
2 tablespoons oil
1 tablespoon cracked peppercorns
2 tablespoons butter
½ teaspoon salt

2 tablespoons brandy
2 teaspoons flour
2 tablespoons Madeira
½ cup whipping cream

Brush each steak with oil and press the peppercorns onto the surface of both sides of the steaks. Heat the remaining oil and the butter in a heavy frying pan and fry the steaks over high heat for 5 minutes on each side. Do not let the butter burn. Season the steaks with salt. Pour the brandy over the steaks and light it immediately. When the flames have died down, remove the steaks and keep them warm. Stir the flour into the pan juices and add the Madeira and cream. Simmer the sauce for 3 or 4 minutes and spoon it over the steaks. The delicious contrast between the pepperiness of the steaks and the rich creamy sauce is the reason that relatively few people become serious vegetarians.

COMMENT: In the directions for making steak flaming in brandy, I have suggested that the brandy will flame predictably if it is heated first. This is true. However, in this recipe, both the skillet and the cooking fat are so hot there will be no difficulty in flaming the brandy directly in the pan.

SIRLOIN STEAK WITH WINE SAUCE

The sauce for the steak can be prepared in advance and reheated.
FOR 2

Preheat broiler.

2 pounds sirloin steak with the bone,
    cut ½″ thick
2 tablespoons oil

Freshly ground black pepper
Salt

SAUCE

1 cup good red wine	4 tablespoons butter
4 scallions, finely chopped	1 teaspoon lemon juice
1 teaspoon cornstarch dissolved in	1 tablespoon chopped chives
1 tablespoon cold water	

Oil the broiler rack and brush the surface of the steak with oil. Season the steak with pepper. Place the top of the steak 3″ from the broiler and broil 6 minutes on each side for rare steak. Add 2 minutes for medium and 4 minutes for well-done steak. Season the steak with salt.

In the meantime, prepare the sauce. Pour the wine into a small saucepan. Add the scallions and simmer uncovered for 10 minutes until only ½ cup of wine remains. Strain the liquid and discard the scallions. Return the flavored wine to the saucepan and add the cornstarch dissolved in cold water. Stir with a wire whisk until thickened. Stir in the butter, lemon juice, and chives. Taste the sauce and season with salt and pepper if necessary.

COMMENT: Do not season the steaks with salt at the beginning of the cooking time because the salt draws the juices to the surface, where they are cooked away, and the meat becomes dry.

≽ HOW TO CARVE SIRLOIN STEAK ≼

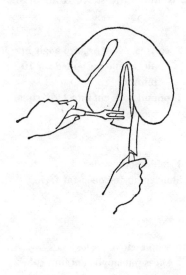

SWEET AND SOUR PORK

This is probably the best recipe ever devised for sweet and sour pork.

FOR 2

If you are using uncooked pork, buy 1 pound pork loin and marinate it for 20 minutes in the following mixture:

¼ teaspoon salt   1 tablespoon soy sauce
¼ teaspoon sugar   2 tablespoons sherry

(When using leftover roast pork, you may eliminate this step, as the texture of the meat is already too firm for the marinade to penetrate.)

Though it improves the dish to deep-fry the pork in batter, this step may also be eliminated if you are in a great hurry. The sweet and sour sauce is also marvelous with chicken.

SWEET AND SOUR SAUCE

½ cup sugar   3 tablespoons tomato ketchup
½ cup vinegar   2 tablespoons cornstarch dissolved in
2 tablespoons soy sauce   ½ cup canned pineapple juice
2 tablespoons sherry

Place the sugar, vinegar, and soy sauce in a saucepan. Bring to simmering point and stir until the sugar has dissolved. Add the sherry and ketchup. Stir in the cornstarch dissolved in pineapple juice and cook for 2 minutes until the sauce has thickened. Remove the sauce from the heat.

VEGETABLES

1 small onion, cut in half lengthwise   2 carrots, cut at a sharp angle into 1"
   and then into chunks ½" wide   pieces and parboiled for 10
1 green pepper, cut in half and then   minutes
   into diamond-shaped pieces   1 pound pork cut into 1½" square
                                            pieces

BATTER FOR PORK

1 egg   1 tablespoon water
2 tablespoons flour   Shortening for deep-fat frying
½ teaspoon salt

FOR ASSEMBLY

2 tablespoons oil   1 whole clove garlic
2 thin slices fresh gingerroot,   2 slices pineapple, cut into cubes
   minced

To assemble the dish, heat the sweet and sour sauce to simmering point.

Heat the shortening for deep-fat frying to 375°. Combine the ingredients for the batter. Dip the pork cubes into the batter and deep fry the pork for 4 minutes until the batter is crisp and golden.

Finally, heat the oil in a wok or large frying pan. Add the ginger and garlic and stir for 1 minute. Discard the garlic. Stir in all the vegetables and cook over high heat stirring constantly for 3 minutes. Pour the sauce into the pan and add the pork and pineapple. Stir for 2 minutes and serve immediately on a bed of rice.

COMMENT: Though the cooking times of all the ingredients are very brief, the preparation is quite lengthy. There are 5 steps to build this dish: 1) The preparation of the sauce; 2) The preparation of the vegetables; 3) The preparation and deep frying of the pork; 4) The cooking of the vegetables in the wok; and 5) The final assembly. None of these steps are difficult, but go over the recipe carefully before you start and you will then know exactly what you are doing.

VEAL WITH LEMON AND BRANDY

The preparation time of this dish is 5 minutes, so have everything ready before you start cooking the veal. Serve it with a fresh vegetable and rice or precede it with a bowl of steaming hot spaghetti dressed with masses of butter, Parmesan cheese, and a dusting of black pepper. FOR 2

¾ pound veal cut for scallopini	1 tablespoon lemon juice
2 tablespoons butter	¼ teaspoon salt
1 tablespoon oil	Freshly ground black pepper
¼ cup flour for dredging	1 tablespoon finely chopped parsley
2 tablespoons brandy	Lemon wedges

Dry the veal on paper towels. It will steam rather than fry unless it is completely dry. Heat the butter and oil in a large frying pan until very hot. Add the veal a few pieces at a time so that the temperature of the fat is not lowered abruptly. Dredge the veal in flour and fry it for 3 minutes on each side. Add the brandy and light it with a match. Remove the veal to a hot serving plate. Stir the lemon juice into the pan juices. Season with salt and pepper and stir in the parsley. Spoon the hot juices over the veal and serve immediately. Garnish the plate with lemon wedges.

COMMENT: This dish can also be prepared with chicken breasts. Ask the butcher to remove the skin and bones and flatten the chicken as though for veal scallopini.

SCHNITZEL HOLSTEIN

This is a handsome dish and tastes as good as it looks.   FOR 2

4 uniform-sized slices of veal cut for veal scallopini	2 tablespoons oil
¼ cup flour for dredging	2 eggs
1 egg yolk lightly beaten with 1 tablespoon milk	2 anchovy fillets, cut in half lengthwise
¼ cup very fine breadcrumbs	1 teaspoon capers
1 tablespoon butter	Watercress
	Lemon wedges

Dredge the veal in flour, dip in egg yolk combined with milk, and then dredge in breadcrumbs.

Heat the butter and oil until very hot and fry the veal over high heat for 3 minutes on each side.

In the meantime, fry the eggs.

Place the veal slices side by side on 2 hot plates. Top slices with a fried egg. Cross the anchovy fillets over each egg and garnish with capers. Garnish the plates with watercress and lemon wedges.

COMMENT: It is customary to serve this dish with mashed potatoes. You really should learn, if you do not already know, how to use a pastry bag, for then you will be able to make the potatoes into a fancy border around the veal. If you have never attempted such a thing before, mash the potatoes with a little butter and milk until creamy but not too soft. Hold the pastry bag in your left hand. Place a #6 rosette tube in the bag and fill ¾ full with mashed potatoes. Twist the top of the bag and press down gently with the heel of your right hand while guiding the narrow end of the bag as the potatoes are forced through the tube. That is all there is to it. Now you can make rosettes of whipped cream to decorate pies and mousses too, as the process is identical.

CHICKEN KIEV

A simply prepared but spectacular dish.   FOR 2

4 single chicken breasts	½ teaspoon tarragon
4 tablespoons butter, softened	2 tablespoons finely chopped chives
1 clove garlic, finely chopped	

COATING

⅓ cup flour	½ cup fine breadcrumbs
1 egg, lightly beaten with 2 tablespoons milk	Shortening for deep-fat frying

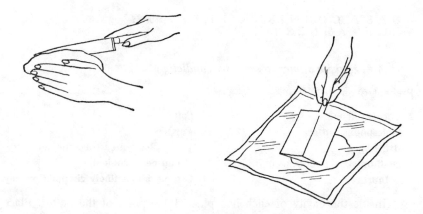

Remove the skin and bones from the chicken breasts and pound them with the flat side of a cleaver until they are as thin as veal scallopini, or ask the butcher to do them for you.

Combine the butter, garlic, tarragon, and chives. Divide the flavored butter into 4 portions. Place a portion on each chicken breast at the widest end. Fold the breasts to form a neat package.
(The breast meat will adhere to itself and it is not necessary to use toothpicks). Chill the breasts for an hour if possible.

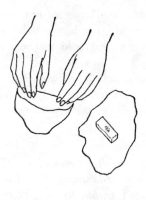

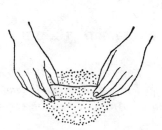

Dip each breast first in flour, then in egg combined with milk, and finally into breadcrumbs.

Heat the shortening to 375° and fry the breasts for 5 minutes until the outside is crisp and golden. Drain and serve with French fried potatoes.

COMMENT: The chicken can be rolled and chilled for several hours in advance of the cooking.

ROAST CORNISH HENS WITH VEGETABLES

An exquisite dinner to serve by candlelight.   FOR 2

Preheat oven to 350°.

2 Cornish hens	Salt
2 tablespoons butter	Pepper
4 strips bacon	1 cup Belgian carrots, cooked
3 medium-sized potatoes, cut into	1 cup peas, cooked
fourths	2 tablespoons finely chopped parsley

Inside the cavity of each hen place 1 teaspoon of the butter. Place the hens in a buttered 9″ baking dish and cover the breasts with bacon strips. Arrange the potatoes around the hens and dot with the remaining butter. Season with salt and pepper.

Place the dish in the preheated oven and roast uncovered for 45 minutes. Add the hot boiled carrots and peas, arranging them around the sides of the dish on top of the potatoes. Remove the bacon strips from the hens and place them on top of the vegetables. Continue cooking for 15 minutes until the breast skin and the bacon become crisp. Garnish with parsley and serve from the dish.

COMMENT: One whole Cornish hen is slightly too large for one person while half a hen is slightly too small. Fortunately, the bacon strips keep the hens moist and so any leftovers are good served cold the next day.

BROILED TROUT

Fatty fish may all be cooked under the broiler, over charcoal, or baked in the oven, while lean fish are best poached, steamed, or fried in butter. Any fish may be exchanged for another within its own category.

FOR 2

Fatty Fish	*Lean Fish*	
Striped bass	Bluefish	Sea trout
Butterfish	Cod	Swordfish
Mackerel	Flounder	All shellfish
Salmon	Haddock	
Fresh-water	Red snapper	
trout	Sea bass	

2 (1 pound) whole trout

FOR BASTING

3 tablespoons melted butter
1 tablespoon chopped chives
1 teaspoon lemon juice

GARNISH

Watercress
Lemon wedges

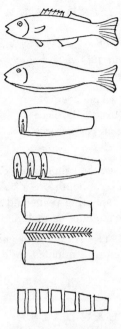

Place the trout on a cold, oiled broiler rack and baste with combined butter, chives, and lemon juice. Place the rack 4″ from the heat and broil the fish for 6 minutes on each side.

Garnish the plates with watercress and lemon wedges.

COMMENT: It is always very difficult to turn fish because the flesh is so delicate. (Thin fillets of fish do not need to be turned.) There are two methods of turning whole fish or fish steaks.

1. Line the broiler rack with 2 pieces of oiled heavy duty foil one on top of the other. To turn the fish, pull the top piece of foil toward you and flip the fish very carefully onto the other side. When the fish is cooked on the second side, lift up the bottom piece of foil and slide the fish onto the plate.

2. Improvise a rack using 2 oiled wire cake-cooling racks. Place the fish on the bottom rack and, to turn it, cover the fish with the second rack and invert the fish and the racks.

POACHED SALMON

Poached salmon with hollandaise sauce, fresh spring peas from the pod, and tiny new boiled potatoes are my idea of a sublime encounter with paradise.   FOR 2

2 fresh salmon steaks
4 scallions, thinly sliced
1 teaspoon peppercorns
1 bay leaf

2 sprigs parsley
1 tablespoon lemon juice
½ teaspoon salt

Place the salmon in a deep frying pan and add enough water to cover the fish by a depth of ½". Add the remaining ingredients. Bring the water to the simmering point and poach the fish gently for 8 minutes. Drain on a wire cake-cooling rack and serve hot or cold with hollandaise sauce.

COMMENT: As a rough guide, a fish that is an inch or less in thickness is cooked in 8 minutes. Add 10 minutes for each additional inch of thickness.

HOLLANDAISE SAUCE

Do not be afraid of hollandaise sauce; the only thing that can possibly go wrong is for the eggs to become too hot. If this should happen, and it will not if you are careful, break an egg yolk into a bowl and add the curdled sauce a little at a time and it will become smooth.   FOR 4

1¼ sticks butter
 3 egg yolks
 2 teaspoons lemon juice

¼ teaspoon salt
Dash cayenne pepper

Heat 8 tablespoons of the butter in a small saucepan until it is hot and bubbling. Remove the butter from the heat.

Place the egg yolks, 1 teaspoon of the lemon juice, salt, and cayenne pepper in another saucepan. Add 1 tablespoon of the reserved butter and place over low heat. Stir constantly with a wire whisk until the butter has melted. Immediately add the second tablespoon of the reserved butter and continue cooking until the butter has melted. Remove the pan from the heat.

Add the hot melted butter from the first saucepan in a slow steady stream, stirring constantly until the sauce has thickened. Add remaining lemon juice.

COMMENT: It is not necessary to serve hollandaise sauce piping hot. In fact the hotter it is the greater the danger of curdling. Serve it at room temperature and the heat of the food will warm it slightly.

NEW ENGLAND SUMMER COD

Not all salads are made with a foundation of lettuce. This one, a variation of a French Mediterranean dish, makes an attractive arrangement on a platter. Black bread and sweet butter are a good accompaniment.

FOR 2

¾ pound cod steak
1 teaspoon tarragon
1 teaspoon salt
1 cup cauliflower flowerets
1 small zucchini

6 cherry tomatoes
1 hard-cooked egg, cut into wedges
3 anchovy fillets
1 teaspoon capers, drained

GARLIC MAYONNAISE

2 eggs
2 cloves garlic, crushed
2 tablespoons lemon juice
½ teaspoon salt

1 teaspoon Dijon mustard
Freshly ground black pepper
¾ cup corn oil
½ cup olive oil

Place the cod in a deep frying pan. Sprinkle with tarragon and salt. Add sufficient cold water to cover. Place on low heat. Bring to simmering point and poach the cod for 8–10 minutes until it is white and flakes easily. Drain the cod and remove the skin and bones. Cut into cubes about 1½″ in size. Arrange the cod in the center of a serving dish.

Simmer the cauliflower in salted water for 10 minutes. Drain and arrange around the sides of the dish.

Cut the zucchini into ½″ pieces and steam in ½″ salted water for 8 minutes until tender but still firm. Drain and arrange between pieces of the cauliflower. Arrange tomatoes and egg wedges around the dish.

Cut each anchovy fillet in half lengthwise and arrange crisscross fashion over the fish. Decorate the spaces with capers.

To make the garlic mayonnaise, place the eggs, crushed garlic, lemon juice, salt, mustard, and pepper in the blender. Turn on the motor and add the combined oils in a slow steady stream. Serve the sauce separately.

COMMENT: Peel hard-cooked eggs while they are still warm and the shells will come off easily without tearing the egg whites. Store shelled eggs in a bowl of cold water in the refrigerator and they will keep for several days.

SCALLOP AND AVOCADO SALAD

If you live near a very good, very fresh fish supply, try this salad. Though raw fish may seem to be a somewhat appalling idea at first, it is often eaten in South America, and as more Japanese restaurants open in North America, it is becoming increasingly popular here, too. Unlike meat, fish is already tender and so only needs to be cooked to become culturally acceptable. This dish is, in fact, a compromise because the scallops "cook" in the lime and lemon juices and turn white and opaque.

FOR 2

½ pound very fresh bay scallops	½ teaspoon sugar
1 tablespoon lime juice	Dash Tabasco
1 tablespoon lemon juice	2 tablespoons finely chopped parsley
1 small avocado, cut into pieces roughly the same size as the scallops	½ cup cucumber, seeds removed, and cut into pieces roughly the same size as the scallops
6 tablespoons olive oil	3 green ripe olives, pitted and chopped
½ teaspoon salt	

Place the scallops in a glass bowl. Pour lime and lemon juices over the scallops and turn them in the juices every hour for 4–6 hours.

Stir in the avocado pieces. Drain the juices from the scallops and stir into the juices the oil, salt, sugar, and Tabasco. Add the dressing to the scallops and avocado. Add remaining ingredients and toss lightly. Serve immediately or the avocado will darken.

COMMENT: Store underripe avocado in a brown paper bag in a sunny window. It will ripen quickly so do not forget that it is there.

❧ HOW TO CHOP PARSLEY ❦

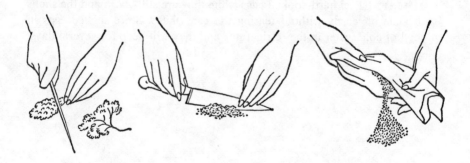

FETTUCCINE

Such a luxuriously glorious dish really must be served with a glass of wine or it is somewhat too rich, if that is possible.   FOR 2

½ pound wide egg noodles
Salt

1 tablespoon oil

SAUCE

2 tablespoons butter
¾ cup whipping cream
4 scallions, finely chopped

1 clove garlic, finely chopped
½ cup grated Parmesan cheese

Bring a large pan of water to boiling point. Add salt and a tablespoon of oil. Drop the noodles into rapidly boiling water and boil for 8 minutes. Taste one to be sure it is tender. Add a cup of cold water and drain the noodles.

In the meantime, prepare the sauce. Place the butter, cream, scallions, and garlic in a small saucepan. Simmer gently for 10 minutes until the cream has thickened and reduced slightly. Strain the sauce and stir in the Parmesan cheese.

Pour the sauce over the noodles and serve immediately in heated bowls.

COMMENT: When cooking all types of pasta and rice, add a tablespoon or two of oil to the cooking water to prevent sticking. Cook pasta in the largest pot you own. It needs plenty of boiling water. Taste the pasta a minute or two before you anticipate that it will be ready. If you overcook it for even a minute, it will be overcooked no matter how you try to convince yourself that it is not.

CHERRIES JUBILEE

Do not believe anybody who says life is not a bowl of cherries. Cherries jubilee are most frequently served with ice cream, but they also make a divine filling for crepes and may be used as a topping for many cakes instead of frosting.   FOR 2

¾ pound fresh or canned black
  cherries, pitted
Grated rind and juice of 1 orange
2 teaspoons red currant jelly
½ teaspoon cinnamon

½ cup cherry juice from the canned
  cherries or ½ cup orange juice
2 teaspoons cornstarch dissolved in
  1 tablespoon cold water
1 tablespoon Grand Marnier

Place the cherries in a saucepan. Add the grated rind, and juice of 1 orange, red currant jelly, cinnamon, and cherry or orange juice. Cover and heat over a low flame for 5 minutes until the cherries are hot. Stir in the cornstarch dissolved in cold water and stir gently until a sauce is formed. Heat the Grand Marnier in a small pan. Light with a match and pour the flames over the cherries.

COMMENT: Cherries jubilee are best made at the last moment. To obtain a clearer sauce, substitute an equal amount of arrowroot for the cornstarch.

STRAWBERRIES ROMANOFF

There are many variations of this dessert, but, to my mind, none better than this. Serve the strawberries with homemade macaroons.

FOR 2 OR 3

1 pint perfect strawberries
1 perfect navel orange
2 tablespoons superfine sugar

1 tablespoon Grand Marnier
1 tablespoon rum

Slice the strawberries into a glass bowl. Add the grated rind of the orange. Remove the remaining white pith and cut the orange into segments between the membranes. Add the orange segments and sprinkle with sugar. Fold in the Grand Marnier and rum.

COMMENT: Any fruit-flavored liqueur may be added to the strawberries, or it can be left out entirely.

COMMENT: Never soak strawberries in water because they will become waterlogged and lose all their flavor. Rinse them quickly under cold running water. For the same reason, do not buy locally grown strawberries after a heavy rainfall.

MACAROONS

Homemade macaroons last for several days and are an extra treat to serve with creamy desserts, fruits, or espresso coffee. They are made in no time at all and the taste is worth every minute.   MAKES 18

Preheat oven to 300°.

2 cups almonds or filberts, ground in the blender	**½ cup sugar**
	2 egg whites
1 teaspoon grated lemon rind	**1 teaspoon almond extract**

Mix all the ingredients together in a bowl. Line 2 baking sheets with folded brown supermarket bags. Cover bags with parchment paper. Using your fingers or a tablespoon measure, form the mixture into small patties about 1½" in diameter. Place on the parchment paper and bake in a pre-heated oven for 25–30 minutes.

COMMENT: The extra thickness of the paper prevents the macaroons from burning on the bottom.

CARAMELIZED PINEAPPLE

A quickly prepared and elegant dessert.   FOR 2

2 slices of pineapple cut ½" thick or use canned pineapple	**2 tablespoons sugar**
	2 tablespoons rum
3 tablespoons butter	**2 scoops vanilla ice cream**

Drain the canned pineapple if used. Dry the pineapple on paper towels, or it will not brown quickly.

Heat the butter in a large frying pan until it is very hot. Sprinkle the butter with 1 tablespoon of sugar. Add the pineapple and sprinkle with the remaining sugar. Cook over moderately high heat until the underside is lightly browned. Turn and continue cooking on the other side until the sugar has caramelized. This will take a total cooking time of about 5 minutes. Add the rum and light it with a match. Transfer to serving plates and top with ice cream.

COMMENT: Peeled and cored pear halves may be substituted for the pineapple.

INFORMAL
DINNERS FOR TWO

❧ MENU SUGGESTIONS ❧

Guacamole
Broiled Chicken with Lemon Butter and Rosemary
Cheese and Fresh Fruit

◆

Potato Soup
Hot Deviled Beef
Fresh Fruit

◆

Quiche Lorraine
Tossed Salad
Fresh Fruit

◆

Crab Salad
Homemade Bread
Homemade Ice Cream

◆

Mixed Grill
Roast Potatoes
Peach Pie

◆

Baked Bluefish
Ratatouille
Boiled Potatoes
Gingerbread

↘ INFORMAL DINNERS FOR TWO ↙

Informal dinners are Monday through Friday meals at the end of a working day. Often they are eaten, not because you particularly want to make dinner, but because you are hungry and this is the obvious way of solving the difficulty. So, keep everything as simple and quick as possible. A little advance planning helps immeasurably, and willingly offered help is something to be encouraged at all times. Here are a group of recipes that are economical and easy to make. They form the foundation for many other more complicated recipes to be served when time and energy are in greater supply.

GUACAMOLE

Guacamole takes only 5 minutes to prepare and tastes best when it is freshly made. If you feel you must make it in advance, cover the mixture with a thin layer of mayonnaise to prevent the avocado from darkening. When ready to serve, stir the mayonnaise into the mixture. Serve as a dip with corn chips.   FOR 2 OR 3

1 very ripe avocado	2 scallions, finely chopped
1 teaspoon lemon juice	1 small tomato, peeled, seeded, and
½ teaspoon salt	chopped
1 teaspoon Worcestershire sauce	2 tablespoons mayonnaise

Peel the avocado and mash it with a fork until it is smooth. Stir in all the remaining ingredients.

COMMENT: It is worth the time it takes to remove the seeds from the tomato because otherwise they will fall into the mixture and make it watery.

MUSSELS WITH MUSTARD MAYONNAISE

A Spanish appetizer. Canned mussels are available in some supermarkets and many gourmet food shops.   FOR 2

2 dozen mussels, fresh or canned	2 teaspoons lemon juice
⅔ cup mayonnaise, preferably	2 teaspoons sherry
homemade	1 teaspoon tomato paste
2 teaspoons prepared Dijon mustard	

Drain canned mussels. Scrub fresh mussels and remove the "beards." Steam fresh mussels in ½" boiling water for 5 minutes until the shells have opened. Discard the empty shell from each mussel and arrange mussels on the half shell around the sides of 2 small bowls.

Stir together all the remaining ingredients and divide between the bowls. Use the mussel shells to scoop up the flavored mayonnaise.

COMMENT: This flavored mayonnaise is also good with raw Belgian endives. Arrange the endives like the spokes of a wheel in individual serving plates. Garnish the plates with watercress and dip the endives into the dressing.

MUSHROOM AND BARLEY SOUP

A slice of leftover beef, cut into small pieces, can be added to the soup.   FOR 2

3 cups beef broth	1 cup finely chopped mushrooms
2 tablespoons pearl barley	(about 8 medium-sized)
1 onion, finely chopped	1 tablespoon finely chopped parsley

Bring the broth to simmering point. Wash and add the barley, and the onion. Cover and simmer for 20 minutes. Add the mushrooms and continue cooking for 15 minutes. Garnish with parsley.

COMMENT: A small electric coffee grinder is a marvellously useful gadget. Throw in a handful of parsley and you will have a sufficient supply on hand to last a week. Wrap the chopped parsley in a piece of transparent wrap. As you have to wash the grinder anyway, make some bread crumbs at the same time. Put in a piece of bread, turn on the motor, and you will have a cup of breadcrumbs whenever you need them. Put the breadcrumbs in a bag and keep them in the freezer.

POTATO SOUP

Ralph Waldo Emerson once said "Nothing is simpler than greatness," and he must surely have been thinking of this soup at the time.   FOR 2

2 cups chicken broth	1 tablespoon finely chopped parsley
1 cup potatoes cut into ½" cubes	½ teaspoon chervil or oregano
1 leek or 1 onion, sliced	Freshly ground black pepper
⅓ cup milk or whipping cream	1 tablespoon butter

Bring the chicken broth to simmering point. Add the potatoes and leek or onion. Cover and cook over low heat for 20 minutes until the potatoes are softened. Mash some of the potatoes into the broth, using a potato masher, and leave some pieces in large chunks. Stir in the milk or cream and the remaining ingredients and continue cooking until hot.

COMMENT: To make vichyssoise, purée the soup in a blender. Add another ¼ cup of milk and ½ teaspoon salt. Omit the butter. Garnish the soup just before serving with thinly sliced radishes.

AUSTRIAN EGGS

This is an anytime-of-day dish. It is very simple and my idea of a farmhouse meal. When there are leftover potatoes, it is quickly prepared and is an undemanding supper to have in bed with the late night movie.

FOR 2

Preheat the oven to 350°.

2 medium-sized potatoes, boiled and sliced	Freshly ground black pepper
2 hard-cooked eggs, sliced	2 tablespoons breadcrumbs
2 anchovies, chopped	2 tablespoons finely chopped parsley
1 teaspoon prepared mustard	2 tablespoons grated Parmesan cheese
⅓ cup whipping cream	2 teaspoons butter

Butter 2 small baking dishes. Arrange the potatoes and eggs in layers and top with anchovies. Combine the mustard and cream and divide between the dishes. Season with pepper. Combine the remaining ingredients and scatter them on top. Bake in a preheated oven for 20 minutes.

COMMENT: Grate ¼ pound of Parmesan cheese at one time and store it in a plastic bag. It is good to keep on hand and tastes better than the commercially grated cheese.

CHICKEN SALAD

A summer salad to be served when the black cherries are at their plumpest.   FOR 2

1½ cups cold chicken cut into
    bite-sized pieces
⅓ cup mayonnaise
 2 tablespoons sour cream or
    yoghurt
½ teaspoon curry powder

½ cup chopped cucumber, seeds
    removed and chopped into pieces
    roughly the same size as the
    chicken pieces
Romaine lettuce leaves
 1 tablespoon slivered almonds
¼ pound black cherries, pitted

Place the chicken in a bowl. Combine the mayonnaise, sour cream and curry powder. Combine the chicken with the dressing and fold in the cucumber. Arrange in salad bowls lined with Romaine lettuce leaves. Sprinkle with almonds and garnish with cherries.

COMMENT: Whenever you plan to serve cold chicken, poach the raw chicken in a pot of salted water with 1 sliced onion, 1 sliced carrot, and 1 sliced stalk of celery for 50 minutes. It will be more moist than leftover roast chicken.

CRAB SALAD

A deceptively simple salad though there are several steps, but all of them are easy. This salad was served at a June garden party at Buckingham Palace. I mention this only because if you should invite the Queen for lunch she may like to have something familiar.   FOR 2

¾ pound lump crab meat
 4 fresh button mushrooms, thinly
    sliced

2 teaspoons lemon juice
2 tablespoons olive oil

DRESSING

¼ teaspoon salt
Freshly ground black pepper
 1 tablespoon vinegar

3 tablespoons olive oil
1 tablespoon finely chopped parsley

GARNISH

1 tomato, peeled, seeded, and cut
    into wedges
1 green pepper, cut into thin strips

6 black olives, pitted
1 hard-cooked egg
6 English walnuts, chopped

Discard any hard membranes from the crab meat and place in a bowl. Add the mushrooms. Combine the lemon juice and oil and toss with the crab and mushrooms.

Combine all the ingredients for the dressing. Toss the tomato wedges, green pepper, and olives in the dressing. Drain the crab meat and mushrooms and place in a mound in the center of a serving plate. Drain the tomato, green pepper, and olives and arrange around the crab meat. Cut the egg into wedges and arrange around the crab meat. Sprinkle the top of crab meat with walnuts.

Serve with crusty bread.

COMMENT: Very often a tablespoon of chopped parsley is needed and, rather than stop and chop it each time, chop half a cup at a time and wrap it loosely in transparent wrap. Store parsley sprigs, unwashed, in a glass jar with a tightly fitting lid and they will last at least two weeks.

SAUSAGE SALAD

Sausage salads are popular in Switzerland, Poland, Austria, and Germany. They can be made with any kind of sausage from bratwurst to frankfurters. Use one or several different kinds of sausage.   FOR 2

¾ pound cooked sausage, cut into slices or bite-sized cubes
8 cherry tomatoes

6 scallions, thinly sliced
2 potatoes, peeled, boiled, and sliced

DRESSING

½ teaspoon salt
Freshly ground black pepper
1 tablespoon red wine vinegar
4 tablespoons olive oil

1 teaspoon prepared German or French mustard
2 tablespoons finely chopped parsley

Place the sausage, tomatoes, scallions, and potatoes in a small bowl. Mix the ingredients for the dressing and toss the salad. Leave to marinate for at least an hour.

Serve with crusty bread or black bread and beer.

COMMENT: If you add the potatoes while they are still warm, they will absorb more of the dressing and improve in flavor.

PICKLED BEET SALAD

A colorful salad to serve with cold sliced tongue and hot boiled potatoes.   FOR 2

4 small pickled beets, thinly sliced
8 paper-thin-sliced red Bermuda
   onions

2 tablespoons sour cream
1 tablespoon chopped chives

Arrange alternating slices of beets and onions on the plates. Top with sour cream and sprinkle with chives.

MIXED GRILL

A marvelous English invention in which there are so many good things to eat you never know quite where to begin.   FOR 2

Preheat the broiler.

4 thin pork sausages
2 lamb chops
1 calf's kidney, cut in half and
   white core removed
3 tablespoons butter, melted
6 slices thick bacon

4 white onions, peeled, parboiled for
   10 minutes
4 mushroom caps
1 tomato, cut in half
2 tablespoons breadcrumbs
1 tablespoon parsley, finely chopped

Place the sausages in a small frying pan. Add ½ cup of water and simmer for 10 minutes until all the water has boiled away and the sausages are very lightly browned.

Brush the lamb chops and kidney with butter and place on an oiled broiler rack. Broil for 10 minutes and turn on the other side. Add the bacon and onions and brush them with butter. Broil for 5 minutes. Turn the bacon and onions and add the mushroom caps and tomato halves topped with combined breadcrumbs and parsley. Brush all the ingredients with melted butter and broil for another 5 minutes. Serve on hot plates with French fried potatoes and the cooked sausages.

COMMENT: Though this looks like a lengthy recipe, it is very easy. All the ingredients are simply cooked in the correct sequence so that they will all be ready at the same time.

SKEWERED LAMB KEBABS

Some of the easiest dishes are the most spectacularly good. Part of the effect with this meal is achieved by serving the food on a skewer. It looks beautiful and is far more attractive than if all the ingredients were put separately on the plates.   FOR 2

Preheat the broiler.

¾ -pound leg of lamb

MARINADE

¼ teaspoon salt	¾ cup oil
Freshly ground black pepper	2 teaspoons soy sauce
1 clove garlic, finely chopped	1 teaspoon rosemary
¼ cup wine vinegar	

1 onion, cut into 8 wedges	1 green pepper, cut into 1½" pieces
6 cherry tomatoes	8 mushrooms

Cut the lamb into 1½" cubes. Trim carefully to remove all the fat. Combine the ingredients for the marinade. Marinate the lamb for 2 hours, or longer if possible.

Preheat the broiler and place the rack on the lowest shelf. Alternate lamb, onion, tomatoes, green pepper, and mushrooms on 2 skewers. Brush all the ingredients with the marinade. Broil for 10 minutes, basting with the marinade once. Turn, baste again, and continue broiling for 5 minutes. Serve on a bed of white or saffron rice.

COMMENT: Leave the oven door open a crack when broiling all meats in case the fat catches fire.

❧ HOW TO CHOP GARLIC ❧

LAMB AND EGGPLANT CASSEROLE

Supper for 2 in a single dish.

Preheat oven to 350°.

1 pound stewing lamb or leg of lamb	1 onion, finely chopped
½ cup oil	1 clove garlic, finely chopped
1 tablespoon flour	1 cup sliced and cubed eggplant
1 teaspoon cinnamon	1½ cups peeled sliced potatoes
½ teaspoon salt	½ cup tomato sauce
Freshly ground black pepper	½ cup beef broth

Cut the lamb into 1½″ cubes and remove all the fat. Heat 2 tablespoons of the oil in a frying pan and fry the lamb over high heat until lightly browned. Transfer the lamb to a bowl. Sprinkle with flour, cinnamon, salt, and pepper. Turn the lamb over and over until coated.

Fry the onion and garlic in the same oil for 3 minutes until softened and then remove from the pan. Add 3 more tablespoons of oil to the pan and heat until very hot. Fry the eggplant cubes in the hot oil, adding more oil if necessary. Fry until lightly browned. Remove and drain on paper towels.

Arrange the lamb, onions and garlic, eggplant, and potatoes in 2 layers in a 1-quart casserole. Combine the tomato sauce and beef broth and pour slowly over the ingredients in the casserole. Cover and cook in a preheated oven for 1 hour. Chill for at least 4 hours.

To reheat the casserole, place in a preheated 350° oven for 30 minutes.

COMMENT: If you have some eggplant left over make a bowl of ratatouille or have eggplant fritters for the next night. If you find that eggplant soaks up too much oil, remember that, the hotter the oil, the less will be absorbed when the eggplant is added.

BROILED CHICKEN
WITH LEMON BUTTER AND ROSEMARY

Also good cooked over charcoal. There will be some chicken left over for the next day.   FOR 2

Preheat the broiler.

2½-pound frying chicken cut into
  parts
Freshly ground black pepper
3 tablespoons butter, melted
1 tablespoon oil

1 tablespoon fresh rosemary or
  1 teaspoon dried rosemary
1 tablespoon finely chopped parsley
2 tablespoons lemon juice
Coarse salt

Season the chicken with pepper and place on an oiled broiler rack.

Combine the butter, oil, rosemary, parsley, and lemon juice. Brush the chicken with the mixture.

Broil the chicken parts except breasts for 15 minutes on each side and the breasts for 10 minutes on each side, basting frequently. Season with coarse salt and serve with corn on the cob and a sliced tomato salad with mayonnaise.

COMMENT: Broil chicken at least 4″ from the heat or the outside will be charred before the inside of the chicken is cooked.

CHICKEN CROQUETTES

A splendid way of serving leftover chicken. Cooked ham and beef can also be used to make the croquettes. Add a teaspoon of mustard for the ham and horseradish for the beef. The croquettes can be served hot or cold and are good to take on a picnic.   MAKES 8

3 tablespoons butter
5 tablespoons flour
1 cup chicken or beef broth
¼ teaspoon salt
Freshly ground black pepper
1 teaspoon lemon juice
1 egg
2 tablespoons finely chopped parsley

2 tablespoons freshly grated
  Parmesan cheese
1½ cups leftover roast chicken, very
  finely chopped
½ cup flour
1 egg, lightly beaten with
  2 tablespoons milk
1 cup fine breadcrumbs
Shortening for deep fat frying

Heat the butter and stir in the flour. Stir in the chicken broth and cook over low heat until a very thick paste is formed. Season with salt and pepper. Stir in the lemon juice, egg, parsley and Parmesan cheese. Stir in the chicken and spread onto a plate. Leave to cool. Cut the mixture into 8 equal parts.

Roll the mixture into 8 cylinders 3" long and 1" in diameter. Roll each cylinder first into flour, then in egg combined with milk, and finally into breadcrumbs.

Heat the shortening to 375° and fry the croquettes 3 or 4 at a time for 4 minutes until the coating is crisp and golden.

COMMENT: Always heat shortening for deep frying to 375°. At this temperature a seal is formed around the food and the fat cannot penetrate to the center. Thus the fried food will really be fat free, just as the advertisements claim.

CHICKEN HASH

An economical brunch or lunch dish, the hash can also be made with corned beef or other finely chopped leftover meats.   FOR 2

2 tablespoons butter	Freshly ground black pepper
1 small onion, finely chopped	1 tablespoon finely chopped
2 tablespoons flour	parsley
¾ cup milk	¼ teaspoon oregano
½ cup mashed potatoes	1½ cups leftover roast chicken cut
½ teaspoon salt	into dice

Heat the butter and fry the onion for 3 minutes. Stir in the flour and add the milk gradually. Stir in the mashed potatoes, salt, pepper, parsley, oregano, and chicken. Fry for 10 minutes and loosen the bottom of the hash with a flexible spatula. Slide the hash onto a large plate and invert back into the frying pan. Fry the second side for 10 minutes.

COMMENT: If you are not insistent on having a perfect pancake of chicken hash, the mixture may simply be stirred in the frying pan until it is lightly browned.

CHICKEN BREASTS
WITH HAM AND CHEESE

Also known as Chicken Cordon Bleu, the dish can be assembled several hours before it is cooked. FOR 2

Breasts from 2 chickens
  4 slices prosciutto or thinly sliced
    boiled ham
  4 slices Swiss, Gruyère, or
    Mozzarella cheese
½ cup flour

1 egg combined with 2 tablespoons
  milk
½ cup fine breadcrumbs
2 tablespoons butter
1 tablespoon oil

Cut each breast in half to make four single breasts. Remove the skin and bones from the chicken and pound until as thin as veal scallopini. Trim the ham and cheese so they fit neatly into each breast without protruding from the edges. Fold the breasts in half.

Dredge the breasts in flour. Dip in egg combined with milk and finally into breadcrumbs. Heat the butter and oil in a large frying pan and cook the breasts for 4 minutes on each side until the meat is white and tender.

COMMENT: Use fresh rather than frozen chicken breasts for this recipe because the meat is more moist and the texture is better.

CHICKEN LIVERS IN MADEIRA SAUCE

A fast and flavorful main course to be served on a bed of rice. If you add only half the quantity of chicken broth, the recipe can also be used as a filling for omelettes, crepes, or puff pastry shells. FOR 2

½ pound chicken livers
2 tablespoons butter
6 scallions, finely chopped
1 teaspoon prepared Dijon
  mustard
1 teaspoon tomato paste

1½ tablespoons flour
¾ cup beef broth
2 tablespoons Madeira
¼ cup whipping cream
2 tablespoons finely chopped
  parsley

Cut each chicken liver in half. Heat the butter in a frying pan. Add the scallions and fry for 4 minutes. Add the chicken livers and cook over high heat for 5 minutes. Stir in the mustard, tomato paste, and flour. Add the beef broth and stir to form a sauce. Stir in the Madeira and cream. Continue cooking for 2 or 3 minutes until hot. Garnish with parsley.

COMMENT: The chicken livers cook very quickly and will not be improved by overcooking.

HAM WITH PORT AND CREAM

A sumptuous entree with a glorious harmony of flavors. A glass of wine is essential to enjoy it to its fullest.   FOR 2

2 ham steaks cut ½″ thick
2 tablespoons butter
6 scallions, finely chopped
¾ cup heavy cream

2 teaspoons prepared mustard
2 teaspoons cornstarch dissolved in
    3 tablespoons port wine

Trim the ham steaks to remove all traces of fat. Make small cuts around the edges of the ham to prevent the slices from "cupping" when they are cooked.

Heat the butter in a large frying pan and add the scallions and ham. Cover and cook over low heat for 10 minutes, taking great care not to let the butter burn. Remove the lid and add the cream. Stir in the mustard and the cornstarch dissolved in the port. Heat until the sauce has thickened.

COMMENT: Canned ham is ideal for this dish. Serve it with a Purée of Peas (given below). The whole thing is incredibly rich, and the pickles, which may seem like an odd addition, were included to give the purée a contrasting taste and texture.

PURÉE OF PEAS

FOR 2

1½ cups fresh or frozen peas
 2 tablespoons butter
 1 tablespoon cornstarch dissolved
     in 2 tablespoons cold water
 2 tablespoons mayonnaise

¼ teaspoon salt
¼ teaspoon sugar
 2 tablespoons sweet gherkins,
     finely chopped

Cook the peas until tender. Drain and force through a strainer. Heat the butter in a small saucepan, add the peas, and stir in the remaining ingredients. Stir over low heat until hot.

BAKED BLUEFISH

A quickly prepared and extraordinarily good-tasting dish. It can be made in the same way with other fish such as snapper, cod, and haddock.

FOR 2

Preheat oven to 350°.

¾ pound bluefish	2 tablespoons finely chopped parsley
4 scallions, finely chopped	2 tablespoons butter
2-ounce jar chopped pimientos, drained	1 tablespoon lemon juice

Place the bluefish on a piece of aluminum foil large enough to enclose it completely. Cover the fish with all the remaining ingredients. Fold the edges of the foil together to form a neat package, making sure that none of the juices can escape. Place the package on a baking sheet and bake in a preheated oven for 15 minutes. Serve with boiled potatoes and a salad.

COMMENT: Thin-skinned lemons contain more juice than the thick skinned variety. To obtain just a squeeze of lemon juice, make a hole in the top of the lemon with your thumb. Squeeze out a small amount and seal the hole with butter. In this way the lemon will stay fresh and may be used several times.

COD WITH AVOCADO SAUCE OR GREEN MAYONNAISE

If you have just a small amount of leftover poached fish, make only half of the quantity of the sauce and have it as an appetizer rather than a main course. Use the other half of the avocado to make Guacamole.   FOR 2

¾ pound cod steaks	2 sprigs parsley
1 tablespoon lemon juice	4 Boston lettuce leaves
4 peppercorns	

GARNISH

6 strips pimiento	1 teaspoon capers

AVOCADO SAUCE

1 medium-sized ripe avocado	Dash Tabasco sauce
1 teaspoon lemon juice	1 tablespoon white vermouth
2 tablespoons oil	¼ cup mayonnaise
¼ teaspoon salt	

Place the cod in a deep frying pan. Add sufficient cold water to cover the fish. Add the lemon juice, peppercorns, and parsley. Bring to simmering point and poach the fish for 8–10 minutes until white and opaque. Drain the fish and leave to cool. Cut the lettuce leaves into thin strips and lay the fish in the center of the lettuce strips. Garnish fish with pimiento and capers.

To prepare the sauce, force the avocado through a strainer to form a purée. Stir in all the remaining ingredients and serve the sauce separately. Or prepare Green Mayonnaise (given below).

COMMENT: If the sauce is not served immediately, it will darken. To prevent this from happening, place the avocado pit in the bowl with the sauce and cover with a thin layer of mayonnaise to form a seal. When ready to serve, remove the pit and stir the mayonnaise into the sauce.

GREEN MAYONNAISE

For hard-cooked eggs and cold fish dishes.

¼ package frozen chopped spinach	2 egg yolks
¼ cup parsley	½ teaspoon salt
¼ cup watercress leaves	Freshly ground pepper
1 tablespoon chives	Grated rind and juice of 1 lemon
½ teaspoon dried tarragon	¾ cup salad oil
1 egg	

Bring ½ cup water to boiling point in a small saucepan. Add frozen spinach and cook for 3 minutes until thawed. Add parsley, watercress, chives, and tarragon. Simmer for 2 more minutes. Drain and pat ingredients dry on paper towels. Place in a blender.

Add egg, egg yolks, salt, pepper, grated lemon rind, and lemon juice. Blend to form a purée. Leave the motor on and add the oil in a slow, steady stream until all the oil has been absorbed.

SOFT-SHELL CRABS

The best way to cook soft-shell crabs is to fry them in deep fat. Serve them with French fried potatoes, coleslaw, and cherry tomatoes and they make a splendid informal dinner. FOR 2

6 soft-shell crabs, cleaned	2 teaspoons paprika
1 cup flour	½ cup milk
1 teaspoon salt	Shortening for deep fat frying
Freshly ground black pepper	

Dry the crabs on paper towels. Combine the flour, salt, pepper, and paprika and dip the crabs first into the seasoned flour, then into milk, and finally in the seasoned flour again.

Heat the shortening to 375° and fry the crabs for 6 minutes. Drain well on paper towels, tipping them to be sure all the shortening has drained.

COMMENT: Jumbo shrimp and tiny Alaska lobster tails can be cooked in the same way.

STUFFED GREEN PEPPERS

An economical supper and a good way to use small quantities of leftover meat. Serve the peppers with a fresh tomato sauce. FOR 2

Preheat oven to 350°.

2 green peppers	¼ cup beef broth
⅓ cup cooked rice	¼ teaspoon marjoram
2 scallions, finely chopped	½ cup diced lamb, beef, or chicken
1 teaspoon tomato paste	¼ teaspoon salt

Remove a slice from the top of each green pepper. Scoop out the seeds and membranes, taking care not to pierce the shells. Combine all the stuffing ingredients, adding only sufficient beef broth to moisten the rice. Replace the slice of pepper to form a lid.

Place the stuffed peppers in a baking dish and fill to a depth of ½″ with hot water. Bake in a preheated oven for 50 minutes until the peppers are soft.

COMMENT: There are so many variations in the sizes and shapes of vegetables that the quantity of ingredients given is of necessity only a guide to which you must add or subtract your own common sense.

STUFFED EGGPLANT

To serve with sliced roast chicken. FOR 2

1 medium-sized eggplant	Freshly ground black pepper
1½ teaspoons salt	1 tomato, peeled, seeded, and
⅓ cup olive oil	chopped
1 onion, finely chopped	2 teaspoons basil if fresh, 1 teaspoon
1 clove garlic, finely chopped	if dried
¾ cup ground beef or finely	⅓ cup tomato sauce
chopped leftover meat	½ cup Swiss cheese, cubed

Cut the eggplant in half lengthwise. Scoop out the flesh with a grapefruit spoon, taking great care not to pierce the shell. Chop the eggplant into ½″ cubes and sprinkle with salt. Leave to stand for 10 minutes to drain out the bitter juices and pat dry on paper towels.

Heat the oil in a large frying pan and fry the onion and garlic for 5 minutes. Increase the heat and fry the eggplant over high heat for 5 minutes until lightly browned. Add the ground beef, pepper, tomato, and basil, and cook over moderate heat until all the fat has rendered from the beef. Drain and divide the mixture between the eggplant shells. Add the tomato sauce and top with cheese. Place in a baking dish and fill to a depth of 1″ with hot water. Cover with aluminum foil and bake in a preheated 350° oven for 35 minutes.

COMMENT: Eggplants are good stuffed with small amounts of cooked meats and rice or with a variety of vegetables. Cook the vegetables briefly before filling into the shells.

CROQUE MONSIEUR

No ham and cheese sandwich could taste better than this. Serve it at any time of the day, for lunch or a midnight snack. FOR 2

4 slices good quality sandwich bread	2 eggs combined with 2 tablespoons
2 teaspoons mustard	light cream or milk
4 slices boiled ham	2 tablespoons butter
4 slices Swiss or Gruyère cheese	2 tablespoons oil
	Hollandaise Sauce (see Index)

Spread one side of the bread with a teaspoon of mustard and make a sandwich with 2 slices each of the ham and cheese. Cut off the crusts and trim the ham and cheese to fit the bread exactly.

Dip the top and bottom of each sandwich in the eggs combined with cream or milk. Fry the sandwiches in combined hot butter and oil as though making French toast. Top with hollandaise sauce.

COMMENT: To make a more substantial sandwich, add crab meat, shrimp, or chicken moistened with a little hollandaise or add mushrooms fried in butter.

DINNERS FOR FOUR

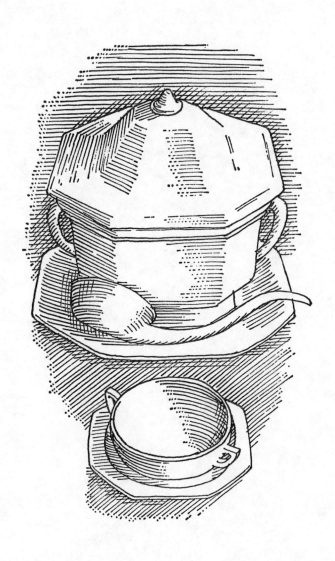

❧ MENU SUGGESTIONS ❧

Cheese Soufflé
Roast Duck with Peach Chutney
Caramel Custard

◆

Onion Pie
Beef Strips in Red Wine
Orange Cream

◆

Marinated Mushrooms
Fried Chicken in a Basket
Eggplant Fritters
Mixed Fruit Pie

◆

Seafood Crepes
Curried Lamb
Rhubarb Cream

◆

Spinach Quiche
Flounder Poached in Cider
Homemade Ice Cream

◆

Roast Chicken with Stuffing
Giblet Gravy
Blueberry Crepes

❧ DINNERS FOR FOUR ❧

Some people set themselves impossibly high levels of achievement. They hesitate to invite two others for dinner because, they say, there is so little time at the end of the day for making a "serious" dinner. Yet guests come primarily for the company, and there are few good friends who would not be delighted to share a bowl of good spaghetti or a simple roast chicken. It does not take any more time, or barely any more time, to make dinner for four than it does for two, so do not let the opportunities slip by using this excuse or waiting for the new couch to arrive.

ONION PIE

This is a traditional English farmhouse dish. Though there are few ingredients, the pie is full of flavor.   FOR 4

Preheat oven to 400°.

PASTRY

1 cup sifted all-purpose flour	1 egg
¼ teaspoon salt	2 tablespoons cold water
¼ cup butter, cut into small pieces	

FILLING

3 tablespoons butter or margarine	Freshly ground black pepper
6 medium-sized yellow onions, cut into thin rings	Dash nutmeg
	3 egg yolks
¼ teaspoon salt	⅔ cup heavy cream

Measure flour into a bowl. Add salt. Combine butter with the flour, using a pastry blender or fingertips. Add egg and water. Stir with a fork, and form pastry into a ball. Wrap in wax paper and chill for 1 hour. Roll out the pastry and fit it into an 8″ pie plate, flan ring, or quiche tin.

Fry onions in hot butter over moderate heat. Cover skillet and simmer onions for 30 minutes, stirring occasionally. Season onions with salt, pepper, and nutmeg. Combine egg yolks and cream with a fork and add to the onions. Remove from the heat and fill into pastry shell. Bake in a 400° oven for 30 minutes. Serve hot.

COMMENT: Onion pie can be made with leeks, too.

BEEF STROGANOFF

You may be surprised at the number of recipes for filet of beef that have been included in this collection. I know it really is very expensive, but it is dependably excellent, and if you can make a splendid meal at home in only a few minutes, it will ultimately cost less and be quicker than going out to a restaurant for a spaghetti dinner. Beef Stroganoff takes only about 15 minutes to prepare. FOR 4

1½ pounds filet of beef
1 tablespoon oil
1 tablespoon butter
1 onion, finely chopped
1 clove garlic, finely chopped
1 cup sliced mushrooms
2 tablespoons flour
1 teaspoon paprika

1¼ cups beef broth
1 teaspoon tomato paste
½ teaspoon Bovril (optional)
½ teaspoon marjoram
1 cup sour cream
2 tablespoons finely chopped parsley

Trim the beef and cut it into thin strips about 1½″ in length and ½″ thick. Heat the oil and butter and fry the beef over high heat for 4 minutes until it has browned. Remove the beef.

Lower the heat and fry the onion and garlic in the same pan for 3 minutes. Add the mushrooms. Cook until the mushrooms are lightly browned. Stir in the flour and paprika and add the beef broth gradually, stirring to form a thick sauce. Add the tomato paste, Bovril, and marjoram. Add the sour cream a little at a time. Do not let the sauce become too hot or the cream will curdle. Return the beef to the pan and continue cooking until the beef is hot. Garnish with parsley and serve on a bed of rice.

COMMENT: The beef will be cooked in the initial frying period and needs only to be reheated. Do be careful not to overcook it or it will be tough and tasteless. Bovril is a highly concentrated beef extract and gives an extraordinary boost of flavor to many sauces, stews, and soups. It is made in England and comes in a small jar. It can usually be found among the supermarket delicacies. Store it in the refrigerator after opening; it will keep indefinitely.

BEEF STRIPS IN RED WINE

Beef stews are made with so many variations they are a constant challenge to the inventiveness of the cook. However, I do not think much can be done to improve this one. Though the list of ingredients looks formidable, in fact all that is happening is that the beef is being cooked in bacon fat, the brandy is flamed to produce an essence of flavor while the alcohol burns off the fat, and a sauce is built around the beef. Finally the stew is garnished with onions and mushrooms. FOR 4

Preheat the oven to 350°.

3 slices bacon, cut into tiny pieces	1 bay leaf
2 pounds round or boneless chuck steak	½ teaspoon thyme
	2 sprigs parsley
2 tablespoons brandy	¾ teaspoon salt
1 onion, finely chopped	Freshly ground black pepper
1 clove garlic, finely chopped	8 small white onions
4 carrots, sliced	8 button mushrooms
2 tablespoons flour	2 tablespoons butter
¾ cup red wine	2 tablespoons finely chopped parsley
¾ cup beef broth	

Fry the bacon in a large pan until it is crisp and all the fat has rendered. Remove and drain the bacon.

Trim the beef to remove any traces of fat. Cut into 1½″ cubes. Dry the cubes on paper towels so they will brown rapidly. Fry the beef, a few pieces at a time, in the hot bacon fat. Add the brandy. Light it with a match. Leave the flames to die down and transfer all the beef cubes to a heavy casserole. Fry the onion, garlic, and carrots in the same fat for 5 minutes. Stir in the flour and add the wine and broth to form a sauce. Flavor the sauce with the bay leaf, thyme, parsley, salt, and pepper. Pour the sauce over the beef. Cover the casserole and place in a preheated oven for 1¼ hours.

In the meantime, peel the white onions and simmer them in salted water for 15 minutes. Drain the onions. Fry the mushrooms in 2 tablespoons of butter until lightly browned. Add the bacon, onions, and mushrooms to the completed stew. Leave the stew to cool and chill it for at least 8 hours for all the flavors to gather themselves together. Discard the bay leaf and parsley sprigs.

Reheat the stew in a preheated oven for 30 minutes and garnish with chopped parsley.

COMMENT: All stews are improved in flavor if they are left to rest for a while and then reheated.

MARINATED MUSHROOMS

The mushrooms are marinated in an oil and vinegar dressing and cost a fraction of commercially prepared mushrooms. Cooked green beans and shrimp can also be prepared in the same way and are handy to keep in the refrigerator to serve with drinks. Substitute ¼ cup fresh dillweed for the tarragon to vary the recipe. FOR 4

½ teaspoon salt
Freshly ground black pepper
¼ teaspoon dried tarragon or
  2 teaspoons fresh tarragon
1 tablespoon finely chopped parsley

4 scallions, finely chopped
2 tablespoons white wine vinegar
6 tablespoons salad oil
½ pound button mushrooms

Place all the ingredients except the mushrooms in a jar. Cover the jar and shake it vigorously until the dressing ingredients are well combined. Add the mushrooms and invert the jar to make sure they are well coated with the dressing. Store in the refrigerator for at least 12 hours before eating.

COMMENT: All French dressings are quickly made by shaking the ingredients together in a jar. They are easy to store without danger of spilling. The recipe may be doubled or tripled so you can keep a 2- or 3-day supply. In spite of the advice of the experts, oil and vinegar dressings do not have to be made immediately before they are to be served.

MEAT LOAF

The addition of cottage cheese gives a light, delicate texture to the meat loaf. Serve it alone or with Homemade Tomato Sauce (on next page). FOR 4

Preheat the oven to 350°.

¾ pound ground round steak
¼ pound sweet pork sausages
1½ cups freshly made breadcrumbs
¼ cup parsley
1 teaspoon oregano
½ teaspoon salt

Freshly ground black pepper
1 egg, lightly beaten
½ cup cottage cheese
½ cup finely chopped onion
3 slices bacon

Place the ground beef in a bowl. Slip the sausage meat from the skins and add to the beef. Place ½ cup of the breadcrumbs in the blender. Add the parsley and blend until the parsley is finely chopped. Add to the meat along with all the remaining ingredients except the bacon. Stir until well combined. Transfer to a buttered 4-cup loaf pan or baking dish. Cover with bacon strips and then with a lid. (If you do not have a lid, use aluminum foil to cover the meat loaf.) Bake in a preheated oven for 1¼ hours. Drain off the fat as soon as the meat loaf is taken from the oven.

COMMENT: The meat loaf can be made with 1 pound of beef, but a combination of meats makes a better tasting dish.

HOMEMADE TOMATO SAUCE

MAKES 2 CUPS

1 tablespoon butter	4 large tomatoes, chopped
1 onion, finely chopped	1 teaspoon basil
1 clove garlic, finely chopped	1 teaspoon tomato paste
1 stalk celery, finely chopped	½ teaspoon salt
1 tablespoon flour	Freshly ground black pepper
2 cups chicken broth	

Heat the butter in a saucepan. Add the onion, garlic, and celery and fry over low heat for 5 minutes. Stir in the flour and add all the remaining ingredients. Cover and simmer for 15 minutes. Remove the lid and simmer for another 10 minutes. Purée the sauce in a blender and force through a strainer to remove the tomato seeds and skins.

COMMENT: When there is an abundance of ripe tomatoes in the summer, it is wise to make several batches of tomato sauce and freeze it in zip bags. The sauce can be used for pasta, stuffed vegetables, and many other dishes.

CURRIED LAMB

The sauce for the lamb can be used to make curry of beef, shrimp, or chicken. Substitute chicken broth for beef broth when using shrimp or chicken.

For an unusual but spectacular presentation, serve the curry in a hollowed-out pineapple shell and garnish the lamb with hot pineapple.

FOR 4

Preheat oven to 350°.

2 pounds leg of lamb, cut into 1½"
    cubes
2 tablespoons oil
1 onion, finely chopped
1 clove garlic, finely chopped
1 small cooking apple, peeled, cored,
    and thinly sliced

2 tablespoons Madras curry
    powder
1 teaspoon paprika
1½ tablespoons flour
1½ cups beef broth
2 teaspoons tomato paste
½ cup raisins, soaked in hot water
    for 5 minutes and drained

Trim the lamb carefully to remove all the fat. Heat the oil in a frying pan until very hot. Brown the lamb a few pieces at a time. Transfer the lamb to a casserole.

Add another tablespoon of oil to the pan if necessary and fry the onion, garlic, and apple for 4 minutes. Stir in the curry powder and paprika and cook for 1 minute. Add the flour and stir in the beef broth to form a sauce. Add the tomato paste and raisins and pour the sauce over the lamb. Cover the casserole and cook in a preheated oven for 1¼ hours until the lamb is tender.

Serve with rice.

COMMENT: Serve the lamb with the traditional accompaniments: popadams, fried in deep fat for 3 minutes, chopped roasted peanuts, yoghurt with chopped scallions, toasted coconut, and chutney.

MARINATED FLANK STEAK

Flank steak is a tough and fibrous piece of beef and is so much better when it is marinated that it is a pity to eliminate this step in the preparation.

FOR 4

2-pound flank steak

MARINADE

1 onion, sliced
1 clove garlic, finely chopped
2 tablespoons soy sauce
⅓ cup red wine vinegar

½ cup oil
1 teaspoon cracked pepper
3 sprigs parsley

Release the tight fibers of the steak by cutting crisscross lines very lightly across the surface with a very sharp knife.

Combine the marinade ingredients in a dish just large enough to accommodate the steak comfortably. Leave the steak in the marinade for at least 2 hours and up to 48 hours.

Preheat the broiler. Remove the steak from the marinade and broil as close to the heat as possible, allowing 4 minutes on each side. Use a timer because overcooked flank steak will be leathery.

Slice the steak across the grain, making long, thin slices by holding the knife at a 45° angle to the beef. Serve on hot plates.

COMMENT: Though the broiler should be preheated, always broil meat by first placing it on a cold rack or the meat will stick to the rack.

The thinner the slices of meat, the hotter the plates must be, otherwise the meat will be cold before you even pick up your fork.

❧ HOW TO TRUSS A CHICKEN ❧

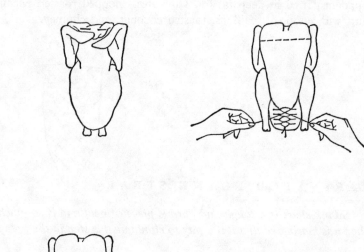

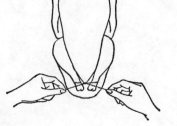

ROAST CHICKEN WITH STUFFING

It is worthwhile doubling the recipe for the stuffing and freezing half of it. It can be used for another chicken or two Cornish hens or served as a side dish for pork. FOR 4

Preheat oven to 350°.

3 tablespoons butter	2 teaspoons sage
1 onion, finely chopped	½ teaspoon marjoram
1 stalk celery, chopped	½ teaspoon salt
1 chicken liver, cut in half	Freshly ground black pepper
1¼ cups freshly made breadcrumbs	1 egg, lightly beaten
4 tablespoons finely chopped parsley	3-pound chicken

Heat 2 tablespoons of the butter in a frying pan and fry the onion and celery over low heat for 10 minutes. Add the chicken liver and cook for 5 minutes. Remove from the heat and chop the chicken liver into small pieces. Return it to the pan and fold in all the remaining ingredients except chicken. Stuff and truss chicken and place in a baking dish. Dot the surface with the remaining butter and bake uncovered for 1¼ hours. Serve with Giblet Gravy (given below).

GIBLET GRAVY

MAKES 1 CUP

Chicken giblets except the liver	½ teaspoon marjoram
½ onion, finely chopped	10 peppercorns
1 carrot, finely chopped	1¼ cups chicken broth
1 stalk celery, finely chopped	1 tablespoon butter
2 sprigs parsley	1 tablespoon flour
1 bay leaf	2 teaspoons lemon juice

Place the giblets, onion, carrot, celery, parsley, bay leaf, marjoram, peppercorns, and chicken broth in a saucepan. Simmer uncovered over low heat for 1 hour. Strain the broth.

Heat the butter and stir in the flour. Add the strained broth. Stir with a wire whisk until smooth. Stir in the lemon juice.

COMMENT: The chicken liver is not added to the ingredients for the gravy because it makes the broth cloudy and too strongly flavored. The cooked giblets may be chopped and returned to the sauce.

HOW TO CARVE A CHICKEN

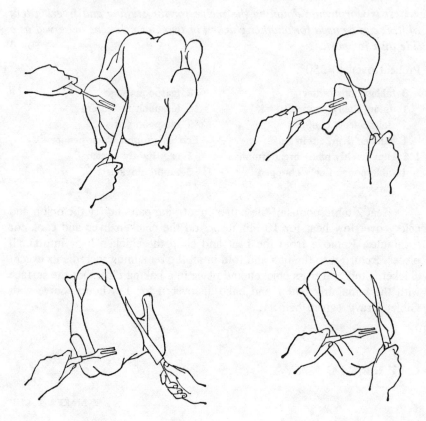

EGGPLANT FRITTERS

Put the eggplant fritters on a large hot plate and they will disappear before anybody touches a fork to the meat.　　　　　FOR 4

1 medium-sized eggplant

BATTER

1 cup flour	**1 cup beer**
1 teaspoon double-acting baking	**Shortening for deep-fat frying**
**　powder**	**Salt**
1 teaspoon paprika	**Pepper**

Cut the eggplant into ½″ slices and into thin strips.

Combine the flour, baking powder, and paprika in a bowl. Stir in the beer with a wire whisk to make a thick, smooth batter.

Heat the shortening to 375°. Dip the eggplant strips into the batter and deep-fry for 5 minutes. Drain the fritters. Allow the shortening to regain its original temperature and fry the fritters for 2 more minutes until the batter is crisp. Drain on paper towels and sprinkle with salt and pepper. Serve immediately.

COMMENT: Do not arrange fried foods in a heaping pile because steam will form, causing the batter to lose its crispness.

FRIED CHICKEN IN A BASKET

The batter for this fried chicken stays crisp even when the chicken is cold.   FOR 4

3½-pound frying chicken cut into parts

½ cup flour for dredging

BATTER

¾ cup milk
1 egg
1 tablespoon melted butter or oil
1 cup sifted flour

½ teaspoon salt
1 tablespoon paprika
Shortening for deep-fat frying

Dredge the chicken in flour and shake off the excess flour.

Combine the ingredients for the batter in a blender or stir with a wire whisk until smooth.

Heat the shortening to 375°. Dip the chicken legs in the batter and deep-fry for 30 minutes. Fry the breasts for 25 minutes. Drain and serve the chicken in a basket with French fried potatoes.

COMMENT: Do not fry too many pieces at one time or the temperature of the fat will be lowered and, as a result, the fat will invade the center of the food, making it greasy and miserable. Solid shortenings are able to reach and maintain a high temperature and are easier to handle than vegetable oils.

CHICKEN IN A POT

A complete dinner cooked in one pot.   FOR 4

Preheat oven to 350°.

3½-pound chicken cut into serving	2½ cups chicken broth
pieces	1 tablespoon tomato paste
2 tablespoons butter	1 teaspoon oregano
1 tablespoon oil	½ teaspoon thyme
1 onion, finely chopped	½ teaspoon salt
1 green pepper, finely chopped	Freshly ground black pepper
1 cup uncooked rice	

Brown the chicken pieces in hot combined butter and oil. Remove the chicken and fry the onion and green pepper for 3 minutes. Place the rice in a 1½-quart casserole. Spread the onion and green pepper over the rice. Arrange the chicken pieces over the vegetables. Add all the remaining ingredients. Cover and cook in a preheated 350° oven for 1 hour until the rice has absorbed all the liquid. Serve from the casserole.

COMMENT: To make a more colorful dish, soak ⅛ teaspoon of saffron filaments in ¼ cup boiling water for 5 minutes and stir into the chicken broth. Garnish the chicken with strips of pimiento or pitted black olives.

MEXICAN CHICKEN AND PINEAPPLE

Chicken with fruit makes an elegant summer supper on a quiet terrace or seated in front of an open window.   FOR 4

Preheat oven to 350°.

½ cup raisins	½ cup sliced almonds
½ cup orange juice, boiling	1 teaspoon cinnamon
3½-pound chicken, cut into serving	⅛ teaspoon ground cloves
pieces	1 cup fresh pineapple cut into
½ cup flour	chunks
½ teaspoon salt	½ cup chicken broth
Freshly ground black pepper	1 tablespoon cornstarch dissolved
3 tablespoons oil	in 2 tablespoons cold water

Soak the raisins in the orange juice for 10 minutes. Dredge the chicken pieces in flour seasoned with salt and pepper. Heat the oil in a skillet and fry the chicken pieces until golden brown on all sides. Transfer the chicken to an oiled baking dish. Add the raisins and orange juice and all the remaining ingredients except the pineapple, chicken broth, and the cornstarch. Bake in a preheated oven for 50 minutes. Add the pineapple and stir in the cornstarch dissolved in cold water. Continue cooking for 10 minutes until the sauce has thickened.

BARBECUE SAUCE

For spareribs and chicken.　　　　　　　　　　FOR 4

2 tablespoons oil
1 onion, finely chopped
1 clove garlic, finely chopped
2 teaspoons Dijon mustard
¼ cup honey
1 cup ketchup

1 cup chili
1 tablespoon soy sauce
Dash Tabasco sauce
4 pounds spareribs or a 3½-pound chicken cut into serving pieces

Heat the oil and fry the onion and garlic for 5 minutes. Remove from the heat and stir in all the remaining ingredients except spareribs or chicken.

Marinate the spareribs or chicken in the barbecue sauce for at least an hour. Broil 4″ from the broiler or over charcoal for 20 minutes on each side.

CHICKEN SALAD

A simple salad for a summer lunch.　　　　FOR 4

2 cups cooked chicken
1 cup boiled ham
2 stalks celery, sliced
1 cup Blender Mayonnaise (given below)
1 teaspoon prepared mustard
1 teaspoon lemon juice

4 small potatoes, peeled, boiled, and sliced
1 head Boston lettuce
2 tomatoes, sliced
1 cucumber, sliced
1 avocado, sliced

Cut the chicken and ham into bite-sized cubes. Simmer the celery in salted water for 5 minutes. Drain and rinse under cold water.

Combine the mayonnaise, mustard, and lemon juice. Fold the dressing into the chicken, ham, celery and potatoes. Line a glass bowl with lettuce leaves. Arrange the chicken salad on the lettuce and garnish with alternating slices of tomato, cucumber, and avocado.

COMMENT: The salad must be prepared at the last moment or the tomatoes will shed their seeds and the avocado will darken.

BLENDER MAYONNAISE

Blender mayonnaise is thicker and consequently a little heavier than mayonnaise made in an electric mixer. However it is absolutely foolproof and is made in 2 minutes.   MAKES 1¼ CUPS

1 whole egg	2 teaspoons lemon juice
1 egg yolk	½ cup salad oil
¼ teaspoon salt	½ cup olive oil
½ teaspoon mild Dijon mustard	

Place the egg, egg yolk, salt, and mustard in the blender. Turn on the motor and add the lemon juice. Add all the oil in a slow, steady stream of droplets. Turn off the motor. Taste the mayonnaise and add more salt or lemon juice if necessary.

COMMENT: If you add the oil too quickly, the egg yolks will get indigestion, a condition that will make itself immediately apparent to your naked eye. Stop the beater at once. Place another egg yolk in a clean, dry bowl. Beat the curdled mayonnaise into the egg yolk a little at a time and it will straighten itself out.

COMMENT: One tablespoon of fresh herbs adds considerable flavor to the mayonnaise. Use finely chopped parsley or a combination of parsley, chives, and almost any fresh herb that may be growing in your window box.

ROAST DUCK WITH PEACH CHUTNEY

An interesting combination of flavors. If you make a batch of Peach Chutney (given below), it will last for a year and tastes good with sliced cold meats. FOR 4

Preheat oven to 400°.

STUFFING

½ cup cottage cheese
10-ounce package chopped spinach,
  cooked and squeezed dry
1 cup freshly made breadcrumbs

5¼-pound duck
2 tablespoons butter
2 tablespoons honey

Combine all the ingredients for the stuffing and fill into the duck cavity. Truss the duck. Place the duck on a roasting rack, and prick the skin with a fork. Combine the butter and honey and spread over the duck.

Roast the duck in a preheated oven for 20 minutes at 400° and 1 hour at 325°.

COMMENT: The duck skin is pricked so that the fat can run freely. There will be at least 1½ cups of fat, so put the duck on a rack in a deep roasting pan or baking dish. The butter and honey keep the duck bathed in moisture and roast to a crisp deep brown, almost black color.

PEACH CHUTNEY

Chutney can be made from any combination of fruits or vegetables. Usually vinegar and spices are added, and occasionally nuts are put in at the last minute before sealing. Chutneys can be served with any cold meats and are particularly good with curry. MAKES 3½ PINTS

4 pounds fresh peaches
1½ cups seedless raisins
1½ cups chopped dates
1 lemon, cut into quarters and
  very thinly sliced
2 cups cider vinegar
3 cups sugar
1 cinnamon stick or 1 teaspoon
  powdered cinnamon
2 teaspoons powdered ginger

Plunge the peaches into boiling water for 10 seconds. Drain and stand them in a bowl of cold water for 10 seconds. Remove the peels from the peaches. Discard the pits and chop the peaches into small pieces. Place in a saucepan with the raisins, dates, lemon, and vinegar. Bring to boiling point slowly and boil steadily for 10 minutes, stirring frequently to prevent the mixture from burning on the bottom of the pan. Stir in the sugar a little at a time. Add the cinnamon stick and continue cooking at a gentle boil for about 2 hours until the chutney is thick. Stir in the ginger and transfer to hot sterilized jars. Seal with melted paraffin wax.

COMMENT: To sterilize the jars, immerse them completely in boiling water and boil the jars for 20 minutes. Drain the water from the jars. Fill the jars with hot chutney, wipe the rims, and add a thin layer of melted paraffin. After the first layer has set, pour in a second layer of paraffin. Cover and store in a cool dry place.

COLD DUCK SALAD WITH ROSEMARY

What a marvelous invention is a duck. When it is served cold it is easy to eat and has far more flavor than either chicken or turkey.   FOR 4

5¼-pound duck, skin pricked with a
   fork and roasted in a preheated
   350° oven for 1¼ hours

2 stalks celery, chopped
2 oranges
12 pitted black olives

DRESSING

¼ teaspoon salt
Freshly ground black pepper
  4 scallions, finely chopped

1 teaspoon rosemary
2 tablespoons red wine vinegar
6 tablespoons oil

Romaine lettuce

Discard the duck skin and cut the duck into bite-sized pieces. Combine the duck with the celery.

Grate the rind from one of the oranges and place it in a small bowl. Cut both oranges into segments, cutting between the membranes, and add to the duck. Add the olives.

Add the dressing ingredients to the grated orange rind and toss with the duck salad. Line a bowl with lettuce leaves and pile the duck salad in the center. Serve at once or the lettuce will wilt.

COMMENT: When serving a cold salad it is good to have one hot dish such as boiled potatoes or hot bread.

FLOUNDER POACHED IN CIDER

Cut each flounder fillet in half lengthwise. Roll it up like a jelly roll to make a more attractive presentation.   FOR 4

Preheat oven to 350°.

1 teaspoon butter
4 scallions, finely chopped
2 pounds flounder, filleted
½ teaspoon salt
Freshly ground black pepper
1 cup cider
2 tablespoons apple brandy

1 tablespoon lemon juice
2 tablespoons butter
1½ tablespoons flour
⅓ cup whipping cream
4 tablespoons Parmesan cheese, freshly grated

Butter a baking dish and sprinkle with scallions. Arrange flounder fillets in the dish. Season fish with salt and pepper. Add cider, apple brandy, and lemon juice. Cover dish with aluminum foil. Place dish in a preheated 350° oven and poach fish for 12 minutes. Strain off the liquid carefully. Keep the fish warm. Melt the butter. Stir in the flour and add the strained liquid and cream. Pour the sauce back over the fish. Sprinkle with cheese and brown under the broiler for 3 minutes.

COMMENT: Almost all fish dishes must be made at the last moment because the timing is so critical the fish tends to become overcooked if it is reheated.

ORANGE CREAM

An almost instant dessert.   FOR 4

1 cup heavy cream
1 cup sour cream
½ cup sugar
Grated rind of 1 orange
⅓ cup strained orange juice

1 package unflavored gelatin
3 tablespoons Grand Marnier or other orange liqueur
1 cup sliced strawberries

Place the cream, sour cream, and sugar in a saucepan. Bring to simmering point and remove from the heat. Add the orange rind. Pour the orange juice into a small pan. Sprinkle the surface with gelatin and leave for 5 minutes. Place over low heat until a clear liquid has formed. Do not let the gelatin boil. Add to cream. Add the Grand Marnier. Pour into 4 glass dishes and chill for 4 hours. Decorate with strawberries.

COMMENT: This dessert can be varied with other fruit liqueurs and fruits.

CARAMEL CUSTARD

An elegant light dessert to serve at the end of a substantial meal.

FOR 4

Preheat oven to 350°.

CARAMEL

⅓ cup sugar   1 tablespoon cold water

CUSTARD

2 cups milk   ½ cup sugar
2 eggs   ⅛ teaspoon salt
2 egg yolks   1 teaspoon vanilla extract

Place the sugar in a heavy saucepan. Add the cold water and place over low heat for approximately 30 minutes until the sugar melts into a light brown syrup. Do not stir. Roll the syrup around the bottom and sides of a 1-quart soufflé dish.

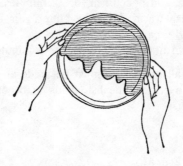

To prepare the custard, bring the milk to simmering point. Stir the eggs, egg yolks, sugar, and salt together with a wire whisk. Add the hot milk and stir to combine. Add vanilla. Pour the custard into the soufflé dish and place in a large baking pan. Add enough hot water to come halfway up the sides. Bake uncovered in a preheated oven for 50 minutes. Remove and cool. Chill for 4 hours.

To unmold the custard, depress the sides around the edges and invert onto a plate with a rim. The caramel will form a sauce around the custard.

COMMENT: Small holes will appear in the custard if it is overcooked. Test the custard by inserting the point of a sharp knife into the center. If it comes out clean, the custard is cooked sufficiently. It will become firmer as it cools.

RHUBARB CREAM

FOR 4

Preheat oven to 300°.

¾ pound rhubarb cut into 1″ lengths	2 egg yolks
Grated rind of 1 orange	2 tablespoons sugar
¼ cup strained orange juice	½ teaspoon vanilla extract
½ cup sugar	½ cup whipping cream
⅛ teaspoon salt	2 teaspoons sugar
½ cup milk	Cinnamon

Place the rhubarb, grated orange rind, orange juice, sugar, and salt in a small casserole. Cover and place in a preheated 300° oven for 50 minutes. Purée in the blender until smooth.

Bring milk to simmering point. Stir together the egg yolks and sugar with a wire whisk. Add hot milk and stir to combine. Return to the saucepan and cook over low heat, stirring constantly until thickened into a light custard. Do not let the custard boil or it will curdle. Cool and stir in the vanilla. Combine the custard with puréed rhubarb. Chill for 4 hours.

Beat the cream until slightly thickened. Add the remaining sugar and beat until thick. Decorate rhubarb with whipped cream and sprinkle with cinnamon.

COMMENT: Double the quantities of custard and cream and use the extra amount to combine with 1½ cups leftover rice to make a rice pudding.

DINNERS FOR SIX

⚜ MENU SUGGESTIONS ⚜

Marinated Salmon
Broiled Boned Butterfly Lamb
Blackberry and Apple Pudding

◆

Crab and Avocado
Roast Pork with Tomatoes and Peas
Cheese and Fruit

◆

Brandade of Cod
Chicken Tetrazzini
Rhubarb and Strawberry Mousse

◆

Watercress Soup
Spaghetti Bolognese
Strawberry Sherbet
Macaroons

◆

Asparagus Quiche
Roast Beef
Cheese and Fruit

◆

Minestrone
Homemade Bread
Apple Pie

⚮ DINNERS FOR SIX ⚮

Dinner for six is rarely a spontaneous event, so there is usually plenty of time to think about the meal, to plan, to prepare, and to get everything in order.

The most important thing about the dinner is for you to have confidence in what you are doing, because if you do not, your uneasiness will pervade the evening, casting a pall of doubt in the room as tangible as an actual disaster.

First decide what you would like to eat, selecting dishes you have cooked successfully more than once before. Make a shopping list or you will undoubtedly forget something and waste time and precious energy returning to the store a second or even third time. Do not attempt to do too much at one time or you will become tired and harassed. Instead, take it slowly a little piece at a time. Then, and this is really important, decide exactly when the dinner will be served and plan the seating arrangements. Finally make a timetable for any last-minute cooking and reheating procedures. Check the table to make sure everything is really ready before announcing that dinner is served.

MARINATED SALMON

This is my favorite of all appetizers. Having been addicted to salmon for years, I discovered that this is, if possible, even better and certainly much less costly than commercial smoked salmon, yet it resembles it closely. The color is clearer and brighter, the texture incomparable, and the taste indescribably luxurious.   SERVES 6 POLITE GUESTS

1 pound fresh salmon steak, as thick	1 tablespoon sugar
as possible	1 tablespoon cracked peppercorns
1 bunch fresh dillweed	1 teaspoon lemon juice
2 tablespoons salt	Toast triangles

Cut the salmon in half horizontally to form two pieces. Cut a piece of aluminum foil large enough to enclose the salmon. Place ⅓ of the dill on the foil. Cover with 1 piece of the salmon cut side facing up. Combine the salt, sugar, and peppercorns and spread half the mixture on the cut side of the salmon. Cover with half of the remaining dill and top with the other piece of salmon, cut side facing down, thus reassembling salmon as it was originally. Cover with remaining salt mixture. Sprinkle with lemon juice and top with remaining dillweed. (It seems like a large quantity of dill but it will be fine. You cannot add too much.) Seal the edges of the foil and place in a loaf pan or dish to fit the package cozily. Weight with food cans. Refrigerate for 48 hours, turning the package every 12 hours.

Open the package and scrape off the salt mixture. Quite a lot of liquid will have formed. Discard the dill and slice the salmon as thinly as possible, holding the knife almost horizontally. Serve with freshly made toast triangles.

The salmon can also be used for making smoked salmon quiche and omelettes.

ARTICHOKES VINAIGRETTE

It has been said that the world is divided into two peoples, those that are addicted to artichokes and the rest. The vinaigrette sauce is a symphony of flavors for hot or cold artichokes. FOR 6

6 artichokes	½ lemon
1 teaspoon salt	

VINAIGRETTE SAUCE

½ teaspoon salt	3 tablespoons finely chopped parsley
Freshly ground black pepper	3 tablespoons finely chopped chives
1 clove garlic, crushed	1 tablespoon capers
½ teaspoon mild Dijon mustard	1 tablespoon finely chopped sweet
2 tablespoons vinegar	gherkins
6 tablespoons light olive oil or salad oil	1 hard-cooked egg, finely chopped

Cut off the artichoke stems very close to the bottom. This will enable them to stand without tipping when they are served. Remove any blemished outer leaves. Snip off the point of each leaf with a pair of scissors, cutting about ¼ inch down each leaf. Plunge artichokes into a large pot of simmering salted water. Add lemon half. Cover and simmer for 45 minutes or until a leaf will pull away easily. Combine the ingredients for the vinaigrette sauce in the order listed. Serve sauce in individual small containers. Serve artichokes hot or cold.

COMMENT: If you wish to remove the central choke, do so with a spoon after the artichoke is cooled. Tie a piece of string around the artichoke so it will keep its shape as it cools. Cold artichokes are equally marvelous with Ravigote Sauce (see Index).

SHRIMP PÂTÉ

This shrimp pâté follows the same pattern as Chicken Liver Pâté (see Index). Similar pâtés are made using lobster and crab meat. Serve the pâté on freshly made toast with cocktails.   FOR 6

1 pound small shrimp, cooked and shelled	Dash cayenne pepper
	¼ teaspoon mace
8 tablespoons melted butter	2 teaspoons lemon juice
¼ teaspoon salt	¼ cup chili sauce

Place all the ingredients in the blender and blend until smooth. Transfer the mixture to an oiled bowl. Chill the pâté for 4 hours before serving. Unmold onto a serving plate.

COMMENT: The final presentation of all food is of utmost importance. The last-minute touches and flourishes form the first and sometimes even the final impression. Decorate this pâté with a single reserved cooked shrimp with its coat still on, and reclining gracefully on a bed of 5 watercress leaves. To "anchor" the pâté, a few more leaves may be placed around the base of the mold but do not overdo the decorations. Garnishings must be delicate, restrained, and very fresh.

CHICKEN LIVER PÂTÉ

Chicken liver pâté is usually served with crackers or freshly made toast at cocktail time, but it is also good for sandwiches made with whole wheat bread and very thinly sliced green apples.   MAKES 1½ CUPS

1 stick butter, melted	½ cup chicken broth
1 small onion, finely chopped	1 tablespoon apple brandy or lemon juice
½ pound chicken livers	
⅓ cup applesauce or thinly sliced apples	¼ teaspoon allspice
	¼ teaspoon salt
	1 hard-cooked egg, finely chopped

Melt the butter and pour it into the blender. Place all the remaining ingredients except the egg in a small saucepan. Cover and simmer for 10 minutes. Pour into the blender and blend with the butter until smooth. Chill and garnish with chopped egg.

COMMENT: The pâté may be frozen.

CRAB WITH AVOCADO

A hot appetizer.   FOR 6

Preheat oven to 350°.

1 pound lump crab meat	2 teaspoons prepared Dijon mustard
2 teaspoons lemon juice	Dash Tabasco sauce
1 tablespoon dry sherry	1 avocado, peeled and cut into
2 tablespoons butter	small pieces
3 tablespoons flour	¼ cup very fine breadcrumbs
1½ cups milk	¼ cup grated Parmesan cheese

Look over the crab meat and remove any hard membranes. Sprinkle with lemon juice and sherry and leave to one side.

Heat the butter and stir in the flour. Add milk gradually to form a thick sauce. Flavor the sauce with mustard and tabasco. Stir in the avocado and crab meat.

Divide among 6 coquille shells or individual baking dishes.

Combine the breadcrumbs and cheese and sprinkle over the crab meat. Put the dishes on a baking sheet and place in a preheated oven for 15 minutes until very hot.

COMMENT: This dish can be made in advance and reheated just before it is to be served; however, do not add the avocado until you are about to put it in the oven or it will darken. Shrimp and scallops can be substituted for the crab, but simmer them for 5 minutes in lightly salted water before continuing with the recipe.

BRANDADE OF COD

This is a Mediterranean dish and may be served as an appetizer with freshly made toast or as a main course with a salad.   MAKES 2 CUPS

1 pound cod	Grated rind and juice of 1 lemon
½ cup olive oil	½ teaspoon salt
2 cloves garlic, finely chopped	Freshly ground black pepper
1 cup heavy cream	12 green olives stuffed with pimiento
½ teaspoon oregano	12 pitted black olives

Place the cod in a frying pan. Cover with cold water. Bring to simmering point and poach the fish uncovered for 15 minutes until it is white and flakes easily with a fork. Drain the fish. Remove the skin and bones and place in the blender.

Heat the olive oil in a small saucepan. Add the garlic and cook for 5 minutes. Do not let the garlic brown. Add to the fish with all the remaining ingredients except the olives. Blend until smooth. Place in an oiled mold and chill for 12 hours. Unmold and garnish with alternating slices of green and black olives.

COMMENT: Salmon also tastes marvelous when it is prepared in the same way. Garnish the salmon with hard-cooked eggs. Force the yolks through a strainer and chop the whites finely.

⊰ BEEF AND CHICKEN BROTH ⊱

Broths are derived from the long, slow extraction of flavor from bones, meat, vegetables, and herbs. Homemade broths elevate all dishes from soups and sauces to stews into full-bodied, rich-tasting, and highly nutritious meals. The process is simple, the ingredients are quick to assemble, and though the cooking time is lengthy, lasting in fact for several hours, the simmering broth requires little or no attention.

If you decide to make a pure beef broth, then, naturally, you would use only beef bones. However, an excellent all-purpose broth can be made by combining both beef and chicken bones. (Lamb bones are used only for making a sauce for lamb or specific soups such as pea soup as they are very distinctive in flavor.) No matter which type of broth is made, the taste will be fuller when raw bones, rather than cooked, are used. Raw bones are first browned in the oven for 15 minutes until they are lightly browned. The browning process not only releases the marrow from the bones but also ultimately gives the broth a good healthy color.

After the bones are browned, they are placed in a large, heavy pan or casserole and sufficient cold water is added to cover them by a depth of one inch. Next the vegetables are added.

The group of vegetables remains the same, whether you are making beef, chicken, veal, lamb, or fish broth. They are known as the aromatic group and include onions, carrots, and celery. Other fresh vegetables such as tomatoes and mushroom stems may also be included, but do not add strong-tasting vegetables such as spinach, turnips, or parsnips as they tend to dominate the flavor of the broth. Use only the freshest of vegetables. Any that have wilted will not improve in taste when they are immersed in the broth and may actually spoil it.

Finally the herbs: parsley sprigs, thyme, bay leaves, and peppercorns are put into the pot along with the other ingredients. Salt is not added at this stage because if the stock is boiled down and reduced it may become too salty. It is best to add the salt when the broth has been completed.

The ingredients are partially covered with a lid to allow some evaporation and concentration to take place. Beef broth is simmered over low heat for 6 hours; veal, lamb, and chicken broths are cooked for 4 hours; and fish broth (made from the head, frame, and trimmings from fish) is ready in 20 minutes. The broth is strained and chilled to allow the fat to rise to the surface. The fat congeals and can be easily skimmed from the surface of the liquid. The broth is now ready to use.

If you are short of space in the refrigerator, the broth can be boiled down to form a small concentrate and be frozen in ice cube trays. It is then reconstituted with water as it is needed. It may be kept in the refrigerator for 2 weeks but must be boiled every third day to prevent it from becoming sour.

VEAL, LAMB, CHICKEN, AND FISH BROTHS

Veal, lamb, and chicken broths are made in the same way as beef broth. Substitute the bones but all the other ingredients remain the same. It is not necessary, however, to brown the bones. Just put them in the casserole and cover them with cold water. Add the remaining ingredients. Simmer the broth for 4 hours.

To make fish broth, use the head, frame, and trimmings from the fish. Cover with cold water, allowing a depth of 1″ above the bones, add the remaining ingredients and simmer for 20 minutes. Strain the broth. It is then ready for use in making fish sauces and fish stews.

BEEF BROTH

Preheat oven to 425°.

2 pounds beef bones	1 stalk celery
1½ quarts cold water	3 sprigs parsley
1 onion, unpeeled and chopped into four pieces	1 teaspoon thyme
	1 bay leaf
1 carrot, washed and chopped	1 teaspoon peppercorns

Put the bones in a roasting pan and place it in a preheated oven for 15 minutes until bones are browned. Transfer the bones to a casserole and add the cold water. There should be sufficient water to cover the bones by a depth of 1″. Add the vegetables and herbs. Adjust the lid so that ¾ of the casserole is covered. Simmer the broth over very low heat for 6 hours. Strain and chill the broth.

PEA SOUP

A full-bodied soup for a cold winter day. Diced cooked lamb or ham may be added to the soup to make it even more substantial. FOR 6

½ pound quick-cooking dried split peas	1 teaspoon sugar
	½ teaspoon salt
6 cups chicken broth	Freshly ground black pepper
2 tablespoons butter	½ cup whipping cream
2 onions, finely chopped	3 slices bread, cut into croutons
1 carrot, chopped	2 tablespoons butter
2 stalks celery, chopped	1 tablespoon oil

Wash the peas and place in a saucepan. Add the chicken broth and simmer for 1 hour.

Heat the butter and fry the onions, carrot, and celery for 5 minutes. Add to the peas and broth. Add the sugar, salt, and pepper and continue cooking for 20 minutes. Purée the soup in the blender. Return to a clean saucepan and add the cream. Cook until hot.

To make the croutons, fry the bread in combined butter and oil over moderately low heat until lightly browned. Drain the croutons on paper towels and add to the soup after it is ladled into soup bowls.

COMMENT: If you do not have quick-cooking dried peas, soak the peas in cold water for 1 hour before beginning the recipe.

MINESTRONE

A thick soup that is so substantial only a light dessert is needed to complete the meal. FOR 6

2 tablespoons oil
1 onion, finely chopped
1 carrot, peeled and diced
1 small turnip, peeled and diced
2 stalks celery, chopped
2 cloves garlic, finely chopped
8 cups chicken broth

¼ teaspoon saffron filaments
1 cup macaroni shells
3 tomatoes, peeled, seeded, and chopped
½ teaspoon oregano
1 cup finely grated Parmesan cheese

Heat the oil in a large saucepan. Add the onion, carrot, turnip, celery, and garlic and fry over low heat for 5 minutes. Add the chicken broth and saffron and simmer for 15 minutes. Add the macaroni, tomatoes and oregano. Simmer for 10 minutes until the macaroni is cooked to your taste. Serve the Parmesan cheese separately.

COMMENT: Peas and other vegetables may be added to the soup, and if you do not have any macaroni, substitute broken spaghetti.

WATERCRESS SOUP

A glorious soup and one that can be made from very simple ingredients. FOR 6

1 bunch watercress
2 tablespoons butter
1 onion, finely chopped
1 stalk celery, chopped
2 medium-sized potatoes, cubed

3 cups chicken broth, simmering
1 tablespoon lemon juice
½ teaspoon salt
Freshly ground black pepper
½ cup heavy cream

Wash the watercress. Reserve ½ cup of the leaves. Chop the remaining leaves and stems into small pieces. Melt the butter in a saucepan and fry the onion and celery for 3 minutes. Add the watercress, potatoes, chicken broth, lemon juice, salt, and pepper. Cover and simmer for 30 minutes. Purée the soup in a blender and return to a clean saucepan. Add the cream and heat to simmering point. Add the reserved watercress leaves and serve hot or cold.

COMMENT: Using this soup as a pattern, substitute 1 pound each of tomatoes, carrots, broccoli, cauliflower, fresh peas, or other fresh vegetables and you can make a vast collection of soups.

BROILED BONED BUTTERFLY LAMB

Ask the butcher to "butterfly" a leg of lamb. He will give you a wide, flat piece of meat that will cook under the broiler or over charcoal in 40 minutes. A 6-pound leg of lamb will serve 6 people when the bone has been removed. Save the bone and use it for soup.   FOR 6

**6-pound leg of lamb, bone removed
    before weighing**

MARINADE

1 onion, finely chopped	2 sprigs parsley
2 cloves garlic, finely chopped	½ cup oil
1 teaspoon salt	1 cup vinegar
1 teaspoon peppercorns	2 tablespoons soy sauce
1 teaspoon rosemary	

Combine all the ingredients for the marinade in a baking dish just large enough to hold the lamb. Marinate the lamb for 6 hours or longer. Turn the lamb at least once.

Preheat the broiler. Take the lamb from the marinade and place 4″ from the heat. Cook for 20 minutes on each side, brushing with the marinade every 10 minutes.

COMMENT: If you want to cook only part of the lamb, use the remainder for shish-kebabs or for any other lamb recipe.

POTATOES SIMMERED IN CREAM

A sumptuous accompaniment for lamb.   FOR 6

Preheat oven to 350°.

5 large baking potatoes	½ teaspoon salt
2 cups whipping cream	⅓ cup grated Parmesan cheese
2 tablespoons butter	Freshly ground black pepper
2 cloves garlic, crushed	

Peel the potatoes and cut into very thin, uniform slices. Simmer the cream, butter, garlic, and salt in a small saucepan until the quantity has reduced to 1½ cups. Butter a small casserole and arrange the potatoes in layers. Between each layer add a little Parmesan cheese and freshly ground black pepper. Pour the reduced cream over the potatoes. Cover with a tightly fitting lid and place in the oven for 1¼ hours until the potatoes are tender.

COMMENT: Though the potatoes are thinly sliced, they take a surprisingly long time to become tender.

BRAISED CELERY

Celery is a flavorful vegetable when it is cooked in beef broth.   FOR 6

Preheat oven to 350°.

12 stalks celery	2 strips bacon, cut into small pieces
1 cup boiling beef broth	1 tablespoon cornstarch dissolved in
1 onion, finely chopped	2 tablespoons cold water
1 carrot, finely chopped	2 tablespoons finely chopped parsley
1 teaspoon tomato paste	

Cut the celery stalks into 3″ lengths. Place the celery in a saucepan and cover with boiling water. Cover and simmer for 10 minutes, drain, and place in a baking dish. Add the beef broth, onion, carrot, tomato paste, and bacon. Cover and cook in a preheated oven for 40 minutes until the celery is tender. Stir in the cornstarch dissolved in cold water and continue cooking for 4 minutes until the liquid has thickened into a sauce. Garnish with parsley and serve from the dish.

COMMENT: Belgian endives may also be cooked in the same way and served with roast beef, lamb, or chicken.

CHICKEN TETRAZZINI

This is a very good version of a familiar dish. I suggest making it in a large quantity because it freezes very successfully and, as it is a complete meal, needs no other accompaniments.   FOR 6

2 2½-pound chickens	2 tablespoons white vermouth or
2 cups chicken broth	dry sherry
2 onions, finely chopped	½ tablespoon salt
2 carrots, diced	Freshly ground black pepper
2 stalks celery, sliced	1 pound thin spaghetti, broken into
1 bay leaf	2″ pieces and boiled for
2 tablespoons butter	8 minutes
6 mushrooms, sliced	¾ cup freshly grated Parmesan
3 tablespoons flour	cheese
½ cup whipping cream	1 tablespoon butter

Place the chickens in a large casserole and add the chicken broth, onions, carrots, celery and bay leaf. Cover and simmer over low heat for 50 minutes. Remove the chickens and discard the skin and bones. Cut the chicken meat into thin strips.

Heat the butter in a saucepan. Add the mushrooms and fry over moderate heat for 3 minutes. Stir in the flour and add the strained chicken broth from the casserole. Add the cream, vermouth or sherry, chicken, salt, and pepper.

Place the hot cooked spaghetti in a baking dish. Place the chicken and sauce in the center of the dish. Sprinkle with cheese and dot with remaining tablespoon of butter.

Place uncovered in a preheated 350° oven for 20 minutes. Serve immediately.

COMMENT: The chicken can also be served on a bed of green noodles or rice instead of spaghetti.

RATATOUILLE

A delicious combination of summer vegetables, ratatouille can be served as a hot vegetable dish or served cold with sliced meats. It may also be put on crackers to be eaten with cocktails.   MAKES 2 CUPS

3 tablespoons olive oil
1 small onion, finely chopped
2 cloves garlic, finely chopped
1 cup diced eggplant
1 tomato, peeled, seeded, and
  chopped

½ cup chopped cucumber
½ cup chopped black olives
1 bay leaf
½ teaspoon oregano
½ teaspoon salt
2 tablespoons finely chopped parsley

Heat the oil in a large frying pan. Add the onion and garlic and fry for 3 minutes. Add the eggplant and fry over high heat until lightly browned. Add all the remaining ingredients and simmer over moderate heat for 20 minutes. Discard the bay leaf.

COMMENT: Other fresh vegetables such as chopped green pepper and sliced mushrooms may be added to the ratatouille. If it is served hot, the ratatouille may also be sprinkled with freshly grated Parmesan cheese.

SPAGHETTI BOLOGNESE

For the greatest visual pleasure serve the spaghetti from a large hot platter.   FOR 6

2 tablespoons oil
1 onion, finely chopped
1 clove garlic, crushed
1 carrot, diced
1 thin stalk celery, diced
1 pound ground beef
3 mushrooms, finely chopped
1 tablespoon flour
1 cup beef broth
½ cup red wine

½ cup tomato purée
1 tablespoon tomato paste
½ teaspoon oregano
¼ teaspoon salt
Freshly ground black pepper
1½ pounds spaghetti
2 tablespoons finely chopped
  parsley
1 cup freshly grated Parmesan
  cheese

Heat the oil and fry the onion, garlic, carrot, and celery over low heat for 5 minutes. Add ground beef and mushrooms and cook for 10 minutes until beef has browned. Pour off accumulated fat and stir in the flour. Add beef broth, wine, tomato purée, tomato paste, oregano, salt, and pepper. Stir to combine ingredients. Simmer uncovered over low heat for 45 minutes until the sauce is fairly thick. Remove from the heat and serve with spaghetti, boiled for 8–10 minutes in 4 quarts of salted water. Sprinkle with Parmesan cheese and parsley.

COMMENT: The spaghetti sauce freezes very successfully.

BLACKBERRY AND APPLE PUDDING

A substantial pudding after a light meal.   FOR 6

Preheat oven to 375°.

3 cooking apples	1 cup flour
2 cups berries (blackberries,	2 tablespoons cornstarch
raspberries, or strawberries)	2 tablespoons powdered sugar
½ cup sugar	1 cup whipping cream
½ teaspoon cinnamon	1 tablespoon sugar
6 tablespoons butter, softened	1 teaspoon vanilla
2 eggs, lightly beaten	

Peel, core, and slice the apples thinly. Combine apples with the berries. Add ¼ cup of the sugar and cinnamon, and place in a buttered 1½-quart baking dish. Beat together the remaining sugar and butter until fluffy. Beat in the eggs. Sift the flour with the cornstarch and add to the butter mixture. Spread over the fruit and bake in a preheated oven for 40 minutes. Dust the top of the pudding with sifted powdered sugar and serve hot with whipped cream (see below).

COMMENT: To make whipped cream, pour the cream into a bowl and whip until thickened slightly. Add 1 tablespoon sugar and continue beating until thick. Add 1 teaspoon of vanilla extract.

RHUBARB AND STRAWBERRY MOUSSE

Rhubarb and strawberries share the same spring and early summer season and taste fresh and interesting together.   FOR 6

1 pound rhubarb	1 package unflavored gelatin
½ cup sugar	1 cup heavy cream, half whipped
½ cup water	2 tablespoons Grand Marnier
1 pint strawberries, sliced	

Cut the rhubarb into 2″ pieces and place in a saucepan. Add the sugar and ¼ cup of the water. Cover and simmer for 15 minutes until soft. Place in the blender. Add the strawberries. Blend until smooth and force through a fine strainer to remove the strawberry seeds.

Pour the remaining ¼ cup of water into a small saucepan. Sprinkle with gelatin and leave to stand for 5 minutes. Heat to simmering point until a clear liquid has formed. Add hot gelatin to the purée and stir in the cream and Grand Marnier. Pour into parfait glasses or a dessert bowl and chill for 4 hours.

COMMENT: Whip the cream until it has the same consistency as the purée. If you whip it until it is very thick, small islands of whipped cream will remain in the purée.

LEFTOVERS

❧ LEFTOVERS ❧

The artful use of leftovers is something of an acquired skill. It is in many ways like a word association game that is played with flavors rather than words. Add one flavor to another and the combination has an entirely new meaning. Leftover egg yolks may enrich a sauce or turn into a mayonnaise, custard, ice cream, or a thousand other disguises. A traditional American steak reappears as a Chinese meal and a stew becomes a soup, a sauce, or a sandwich.

When food is well cooked and carefully stored, it can be equally glorious two or three days later. The skillful adaptation of leftovers make many a surprising economical and interesting meal and are the true test of a good cook. Anybody can roast a chicken, but with a repertoire of dozens of dishes that can be made from leftovers, an inventive cook can explore uncharted territories.

❧ HOW TO USE LEFTOVERS ❧

Wrap leftover food quickly in transparent wrap. Chill and serve the food in a new dish as soon as possible.

Chop and slice leftover foods only when you are ready to use them or the food becomes dry very quickly.

Do not combine a group of leftover foods merely because they all happen to be living in the same refrigerator at the same time. Each ingredient must be added for a good reason or you will end up with a clean, empty refrigerator and a meal that looks terrible and tastes worse.

Add at least one fresh ingredient to a new dish made from previously cooked food and always serve with a different garnish and new accompaniments.

Reheat leftover food briefly. If the food is overcooked it will lose color, texture, and nutritive value. It will also not taste good.

Keep frozen leftovers for a minimum length of time, preferably six weeks or less.

LEFTOVER STEW

A small amount of stew may be reheated and served on a slice of toasted bread as an open sandwich.

Cut the meat into small pieces and add sufficient beef or chicken broth to make the stew into a soup.

Cut the meat into smaller pieces and use as an omelette or crepe filling.

Divide the stew between individual baking dishes and top with rosettes of mashed potatoes. Sprinkle the potatoes with grated cheese, dot with butter, and bake in a preheated 350° oven for 15 minutes until very hot.

Heat 1 tablespoon of butter and stir in either 1 teaspoon of curry powder and 1 teaspoon of paprika, or 1 teaspoon of chili powder and 1 teaspoon of paprika for each cup of stew. Stir the spices into the stew and reheat in a preheated 350° oven for 15 minutes.

SOUP FROM LEFTOVER VEGETABLES

Leftover vegetables tend to lose both color and texture when they are reheated, but they can be made into remarkably good soup. FOR 2

1 cup cooked cauliflower, broccoli, or other vegetable	1 stalk celery, chopped
	1 teaspoon curry powder
1 tablespoon butter	2 teaspoons flour
1 small onion, chopped	2 cups chicken broth

Cut the vegetables into small pieces. Heat the butter in a saucepan and fry the onion and celery for 5 minutes until softened. Stir in the curry powder and the flour. Add the chicken broth and simmer for 5 minutes. Transfer all the ingredients and the vegetables to the blender. Purée the soup until smooth. Return to the saucepan and serve hot.

COMMENT:　The soup will be even better if it is garnished with croutons, grated cheese, crumbled bacon, or tiny crisp pieces of celery.

FISH CAKES FROM LEFTOVER FISH

Leftover cooked fish is combined with mashed potatoes and fried in butter. Though any cooked fish may be used, cod, haddock, halibut, and salmon are the best choices. FOR 2

1 cup flaked fish	1 egg, lightly beaten with
1½ cups mashed potatoes	1 tablespoon milk
1 teaspoon chopped chives	⅓ cup fine breadcrumbs
1 tablespoon finely chopped	2 tablespoons butter
parsley	1 tablespoon oil
⅓ cup flour	Tartar sauce

Combine the fish, potatoes, chives, and parsley. Form into 4 flat patties. Dredge in flour, then in beaten egg combined with milk, and finally into breadcrumbs.

Heat the butter and oil and fry the fish cakes over moderately high heat for 4 minutes on each side. Drain on paper towels and serve with tartar sauce.

COMMENT: Leftover ground meat or chicken can be cooked in the same manner.

❧ FREEZING FOOD ☙

There are many reasons for owning a freezer, but not all of them are valid. A freezer can increase the variety of foods that are readily available. Recipes or portions of recipes can be doubled and tripled so whole preparations may be frozen, or parts of recipes are prepared in advance and frozen. This is a great convenience and timesaver. However, there is a certain hidden cost, not only in the freezer itself, but in the consumption of electricity and in packaging materials for the foods.

While for some the freezing compartment of the refrigerator has sufficient space, for others, who may have access to farm fresh vegetables or fruits, for those who have a source of supply for a large quantity of meat, chicken, or fish, or for people who do a great amount of entertaining, a freezer is more of a necessity than a luxury. (The freezer part of the refrigerator cannot maintain 0°, the ideal temperature for freezing, so food cannot be stored for long periods of time without deteriorating.) If you do decide to buy a freezer, a self-defrosting model is certainly worth the extra cost in convenience.

It is easier to see all the foods at a glance, if you are reasonably tidy, with an upright rather than a chest type of freezer. For the maximum operating economy, a freezer should be kept three quarters full.

Though it is claimed that all foods freeze satisfactorily, it is the opinion of some among us that raw foods, particularly fish and meats, cannot be frozen as successfully as dishes prepared in a sauce and subsequently frozen. This is because there is an inevitable change in texture after freezing and thawing. I believe this to be so and that, in general, the best results are obtained by cooking fresh ingredients.

Those foods that are most successfully frozen are bread, pastry, and cakes except those containing cream. Butter cream, however, is successful in the freezer.

Stews, soups, and sauces, except egg-based sauces, also freeze well. Meats, chicken, and fish prepared in a sauce do well in the freezer.

Fruit purées, fruits and vegetables after a preliminary blanching also freeze successfully, as do mousses, cold soufflés, and puddings.

Hard cheeses and butter can be frozen.

Do not freeze eggs, cream, sour cream, or yoghurt.

Potatoes do not freeze unless they are cooked and become part of another dish, and they are best if they are mashed. Crisp vegetables lose their crispness in the freezer and batter-fried foods become soggy. Apples are best frozen in the form of pies and puddings.

❧ HOW TO PREPARE FOOD ❦
FOR THE FREEZER

Wrap all food in special freezer wrap, preferably transparent wrap. Seal, label, and date the packages. It should not be possible for air to enter or for moisture to leave the package. Unless ice cream is used quickly, wrap the carton in freezer wrap because air can enter even waterproof paper cartons. Put homemade ice cream in specially treated paper or plastic containers. Use square rather than round sloping-sided containers because the square containers can be stacked and take up less space.

Chill food before freezing. Do not overload the freezer with huge quantities of unfrozen food because it takes too long for the food to freeze. Ice crystals form within the packages, causing the food to lose flavor, color, and texture. Add foods to be frozen a little at a time, making sure that the first batch is solidly frozen before adding more.

Efficient people keep a running inventory of the food in the freezer; others say they know exactly what is there and maybe they do. The author neither keeps an inventory nor remembers, but it is good to have a surprise once in a while.

Rotate the food in the freezer by eating some of it from time to time.

⚥ DEFROSTING FOOD ⚥

Ideally, foods should be defrosted slowly in the coldest part of the refrigerator. This will prevent any serious deterioration in the texture and flavor. If this is not practical, stand meats on a rack on the kitchen counter. Brush meats with oil. The oil will prevent, or partially prevent, loss of juices.

Some foods may be taken directly from the freezer and cooked in their frozen state. If the food is raw, increase the total cooking time by half as long again; i.e., if you expect a raw steak to cook in 16 minutes, cook a frozen steak for $16 + 8 = 24$ minutes. Frozen foods can be taken directly from the freezer and cooked in an electric slow cooker (the slow cooking utensil made of stoneware).

⚥ LEFTOVER ROAST BEEF ⚥

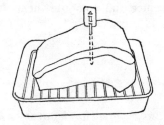

ROAST BEEF

Assuming you have decided to splurge on a luxurious roast of prime ribs of beef, the noble beast will provide you with some precious morsels to serve in a variety of other ways.   FOR 6

Preheat oven to 450°.

6-pound rib roast with backbone removed and tied with string at ½″ intervals	**2 teaspoons salt** **Freshly ground black pepper** **1 teaspoon thyme**

Rub the surface of the beef with salt, pepper, and thyme. Insert a meat thermometer into the center of the meat. Place in a roasting pan and put in the lower third of a preheated oven for 15 minutes. Lower the heat and continue cooking for 1 hour until a thermometer reading of 120° for rare beef, 130° for medium, and 150° for well done (overcooked) beef. This is roughly 13 minutes to the pound for rare beef.

Remove the beef from the oven, untie the backbone, and wrap the beef in aluminum foil. Leave it to rest for 20 minutes before carving.

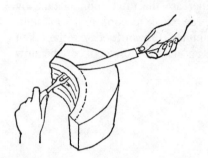 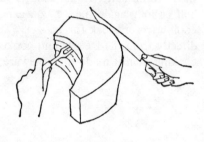

COMMENT: The resting period for all roasts is extremely important. If the beef is carved the moment it comes from the oven, it will be flabby and difficult to cut. If the beef is cut too quickly, the juices will pour from the beef into the well of the carving board and from there will spill onto the tablecloth.

When the beef is allowed to rest, the juices that have risen to the surface return to the center and compose themselves quietly. When the beef is cut it is moist and succulent.

CRISP-FRIED BEEF

This recipe may also be used for leftover turkey and pork. It is so good it is worth cooking an extra large piece of beef in order to have some left over. FOR 2

2 slices rare roast beef cut ¼″ thick	⅓ cup freshly made fine breadcrumbs
¼ cup flour	3 tablespoons oil
1 egg, lightly beaten with 2 teaspoons prepared Dijon mustard and 1 teaspoon Worcestershire sauce	1 tablespoon finely chopped parsley

Trim the beef to remove all traces of fat. Dredge the slices in flour, then in egg combined with mustard and Worcestershire sauce, and finally into the breadcrumbs.

Heat the oil in a large frying pan until it is very hot. Fry the beef for 3 minutes on each side until a crisp golden crust is formed. Garnish with parsley.

Serve immediately.

COMMENT: The three-process method of forming a coating is used over and over again for meats, poultry, fish, and vegetables. The food is first dredged in flour to make a dry surface. It is then dipped in egg, made less viscous with the addition of milk or another liquid (or the food may be dipped into a batter at this stage), and finally into breadcrumbs to give the crisp coating. If you leave out the flour, the egg or the batter will roll off the food and if you leave out the egg covering, the crumbs will fall off, so everything has a logical purpose.

HOT DEVILED BEEF

If you have never tried grated zucchini, it is a beautiful and delicate vegetable. If you would like to serve it alone, heat 1 tablespoon of butter in a saucepan, add the grated zucchini, a little salt, and a small squeeze of lemon juice. Cover and steam it for 5 minutes. Drain through a colander, pressing down slightly to remove the excess moisture that will have accumulated. FOR 2

Preheat oven to 300°.

3 or 4 slices cold roast beef cut into thin strips	1 tablespoon flour
	¾ cup beef broth
1 zucchini, grated, steamed, and squeezed dry	1 tablespoon red wine vinegar
	1 teaspoon sugar
1 tablespoon oil	2 teaspoons Dijon mustard
1 onion, finely chopped	1 teaspoon capers
1 clove garlic, finely chopped	½ cup breadcrumbs

Place the beef in a baking dish and cover with zucchini.

Heat the oil and fry the onion and garlic for 4 minutes. Stir in the flour and add the beef broth. Stir in the vinegar, sugar, mustard, and capers. Pour the sauce over the zucchini and beef and top with the breadcrumbs. Place in a preheated oven for 15 minutes.

COMMENT: Any other cooked vegetable may be substituted for the zucchini.

STIR-FRIED BEEF

When transforming leftovers into new and different dishes it is always more interesting to add at least one fresh ingredient. Leftover flank steak can also be used in this recipe. The idea is to reheat the beef as rapidly as possible, to combine the beef with vegetables, and to build a sauce around the principal ingredients. FOR 2

1 cup cold roast beef, cut into thin strips
1 tablespoon sherry
1 teaspoon soy sauce
1 carrot, cut into thin strips about 1½″ long and ⅟₁₆″ wide
1 celery stalk, cut into slices ⅛″ thick

6 scallions, 2″ green stem and white bulb cut in half lengthwise
1 green pepper, cut into 1″ pieces
2 tablespoons oil
1 clove garlic
1 cup beef broth, simmering
2 teaspoons cornstarch dissolved in 2 tablespoons cold water
1 cup cooked hot rice

Marinate the beef in combined sherry and soy sauce while preparing the remaining ingredients.

Bring 2 quarts of salted water to boiling point. Add all the vegetables and simmer uncovered for 5 minutes. Drain and rinse the vegetables under cold running water. Heat the oil in a wok or large frying pan. Fry the garlic for 2 minutes and discard it. Add the vegetables and stir-fry them for 3 minutes. Add the beef with the sherry and soy sauce. Add the beef broth. Stir in the cornstarch dissolved in cold water and continue cooking for 2 minutes until the sauce has thickened.

Serve immediately with rice.

COMMENT: All the vegetables are interchangeable with other vegetables. Use whatever is available, adapting the idea of the recipe to the state of the refrigerator.

The purpose of stir-frying is to keep the ingredients moving rapidly while keeping them in constant contact with the hot metal of the utensil, preferably a wok. The small amount of frying oil is sufficient to prevent the food from sticking to the pan. The food is cooked very quickly and so retains its taste, color, texture, and nutritional value.

LEFTOVER BEEF WITH SAVORY SAUCE

Leftover beef needs only to be reheated, not recooked.   FOR 2

4 slices leftover beef cut ¼" thick
1 tablespoon butter
1 tablespoon oil
1 onion, finely chopped
1 clove garlic, finely chopped
2 mushrooms, thinly sliced
1½ tablespoons flour

¾ cup beef broth
1 teaspoon red wine vinegar
1 teaspoon tomato paste
2 teaspoons prepared horseradish
¼ cup sour cream
1 tablespoon finely chopped parsley
1 cup cooked hot green noodles

Trim the beef and cut into strips. Heat the butter and oil. Add the onion and garlic. Cover and cook over low heat for 15 minutes until soft. Remove the lid, increase the heat, and fry the mushrooms briefly. Add the flour and stir in the beef broth, vinegar, tomato paste, and horseradish. Add the beef and continue cooking for 5 minutes until hot. Stir in the sour cream and garnish with parsley. Serve with hot buttered green noodles.

COMMENT: This recipe can also be prepared with leftover pork. Substitute mustard for horseradish.

COLD BEEF SALAD

The salad can be made several hours in advance, and, like all cold dishes, it has a fuller flavor if it is not served directly from the refrigerator.

FOR 2

4 slices rare roast beef
¼ teaspoon salt
Freshly ground black pepper
1 teaspoon horseradish
1 tablespoon red wine vinegar
4 tablespoons olive oil

4 scallions, finely chopped
1 tablespoon finely chopped parsley
1 cup cold cooked rice
½ cup cooked peas
1 small tomato, cut into small pieces
Lettuce leaves

Cut the beef into thin strips. Combine the salt, pepper, horseradish, vinegar, and oil. Add the dressing to the beef and stir in all the remaining ingredients except lettuce. When ready to serve, place on plates lined with lettuce leaves.

COMMENT: Many variations can be made in this salad. Substitute or add other fresh vegetables that are in season.

HOT BEEF SANDWICH

Your enjoyment of this sandwich is largely dependent on your attitude toward onions. If you are not fond of them, reduce the quantity and add more mushrooms.   FOR 2

4 thin slices roast beef	½ cup red wine
2 tablespoons butter	1 tablespoon meat sauce such as
2 small onions, thinly sliced	A.1.
1–4 mushrooms, thinly sliced	1 teaspoon tomato paste
1½ tablespoons flour	2 slices firm-textured bread
½ cup beef broth	

Trim the beef to remove all fat. Cut each slice of beef in half.

Heat the butter in a small saucepan. Add the onions, cover, and cook over a low heat for 15 minutes until the onions are soft. Remove the lid, increase the heat, and fry the mushrooms briefly. Stir in the flour and add the beef broth and wine slowly. Add the meat sauce and tomato paste. Add the beef and cook for 2 minutes until the beef is hot.

Toast the bread and cover with the beef in the sauce.

COMMENT: Bread freezes very successfully, so if you can track down a good bakery, buy more than one loaf at a time. It will improve the quality of your life.

⊰ LEFTOVER PORK ⊱

ROAST PORK LOIN

It is impossible to prepare a very small roast because the large exposed surface area becomes dry before the center of the meat is fully cooked. A 2-pound roast is the minimum size that will cook satisfactorily, but a 3-pound roast will taste even better and there are many ways of using the leftovers.   FOR 6

Preheat oven to 350°.

3-pound boneless pork loin	1 teaspoon salt
4 teaspoons prepared Dijon mustard	1 teaspoon crushed peppercorns
1 teaspoon rosemary	

Score the pork fat in a diamond pattern and place on a rack in a shallow roasting pan. Combine the mustard, rosemary, salt, and pepper and spread over the surface fat.

Roast the pork for 2 hours or until a meat thermometer reaches 170°. Allow the pork to rest for 20 minutes before carving.

COMMENT: A boneless roast is easy to carve. Serve the pork with a lentil purée.

ROAST PORK WITH TOMATOES AND PEAS

If you find you do not have any leftover sauce, you can make one quickly and easily and reheat the pork in its new surroundings.   FOR 2

2 slices leftover pork	1 teaspoon soy sauce
1 tablespoon butter	1 teaspoon Worcestershire sauce
1 tablespoon flour	1 tomato, peeled, seeded, and cut
1 cup beef broth	into small pieces
1 teaspoon mustard	½ cup peas, cooked

Cut the pork into cubes.

Heat the butter in a small saucepan. Add the flour and stir in the beef broth with a wire whisk to form a smooth sauce. Add the remaining ingredients and the pork and simmer for 10 minutes.

Serve on a bed of rice.

COMMENT: If you have sufficient freezer space, it is economical to buy frozen vegetables in the large family-size plastic bags. Take out as much as you need and wrap 2 sturdy rubber bands over the top of the bag to seal it again.

PORK SALAD WITH CHUTNEY SAUCE

Firm cold pork makes a tasty salad for the summer.   FOR 2

6 thin slices cold roast pork
1 small apple, peel left on, cored and
   very thinly sliced
4 small cold boiled potatoes, thinly
   sliced

1 hard-cooked egg, sliced
Boston lettuce
½ cup mayonnaise
⅓ cup chutney
4 strips pimiento

Arrange the pork, apple slices, potatoes, and egg slices on plates lined with lettuce leaves. Put the mayonnaise in a bowl. Add the liquid from the chutney and chop the solid parts of the chutney into small pieces. Stir the chutney into the mayonnaise and serve separately. Decorate the pork slices with pimiento.

COMMENT: The mayonnaise may be flavored with 2 teaspoons of mustard if you prefer that idea.

ROAST PORK SHREDS WITH FRIED RICE

A quick and economical main course with the last remnants of a pork roast.   FOR 2

2 tablespoons oil
½ small onion, finely chopped
2 eggs, lightly beaten
1 cup cold pork cut into thin strips
2 cups cold cooked rice

½ cup peas, cooked
1 teaspoon sherry or soy sauce
½ teaspoon salt
Freshly ground black pepper

Heat the oil in a wok or large frying pan. Add the onion and stir over high heat for 2 minutes. Add the eggs and stir until scrambled. Add the pork and stir in the rice and peas. Add the sherry or soy sauce and season with salt and pepper. Stir over moderate heat until all the ingredients are hot and well combined.

COMMENT: Even if you do not feel comfortable eating with chopsticks, they are the best utensils for moving stir-fried food around in the wok.

CASSOULET

A cassoulet *is a regional French dish built on a pot of beans. Among the beans are hidden all manner of treasures including roast duck, lamb, sausage, pork, and even beef, though beef is less often used than the other ingredients. The entire dish is a glorious feast. The following recipe picks up the idea, but in a shortened version. It is an interesting way of using up leftover cooked meats when there is not a sufficient quantity of any one meat to serve 2 people.* FOR 2

1-pound 4-ounce can white kidney
    beans
¼ cup finely chopped onions
8-ounce can Italian plum tomatoes
2 teaspoons prepared Dijon mustard

Cooking juices from a recent roast if available, or 3 tablespoons beef broth
3 thick slices cold pork cut into 1½" cubes or a combination of leftover pork, chicken, etc. (see introductory note above)

Place the beans in a saucepan with all the remaining ingredients. Simmer uncovered for 20 minutes over low heat.

COMMENT: After roasting a chicken or other meat, a layer of fat will be left in the roasting pan. Skim off this layer and beneath it you will find a small quantity of clear jellied juices. Save these juices very carefully. They are as precious as any ingredient you can buy. Add the juices to soups, stews, or sauces. They are rich, flavorful, and highly nutritious.

CHOUCROUTE

Many regional French dishes are based on an idea rather than a precise measurement of ingredients. Choucroute *consists of pork or a variety of pork products such as thickly sliced bacon and pork sausages, Polish sausages or frankfurters. The meats are placed on a bed of sauerkraut. Use whatever meats you have on hand.* FOR 4

Preheat oven to 350°.

1 pound sauerkraut
½ cup white wine
½ cup chicken broth
½ cup applesauce
1 teaspoon black peppercorns

4 slices roast pork or a combination of pork, bacon, and sausages, cooked
8 slices thick bacon, cooked

Rinse the sauerkraut and squeeze it dry to remove all the liquid. Place all the ingredients except the meats in a saucepan. Cover and simmer for 1½ hours over low heat until the sauerkraut has absorbed all the liquid. Transfer the sauerkraut to a buttered baking dish. Top with the cooked meats. Cover with aluminum foil and place in a preheated 350° oven for 20 minutes until the meats are hot.

Serve with a brown sauce.

COMMENT: Whenever a recipe calls for a reheating process, the dish can be made in advance to that point.

PORK WITH LENTIL PURÉE

Some people spend an entire lifetime never finding out how good lentils are. The lentil purée can also be served with other roast meats.

FOR 2

Preheat oven to 350°.

4 slices cooked pork or 4 pork chops

LENTIL PURÉE

½ cup lentils	¼ cup chicken broth
¼ cup chopped onion	2 tablespoons butter
1 carrot, diced	½ teaspoon cumin or curry powder
1 stalk celery, finely chopped	

Slice the pork and leave to one side or fry the pork chops for 10 minutes on each side.

Wash the lentils and place in a saucepan with the onion, carrot, and celery. Add cold water to cover the lentils by a depth of 2". Cover and simmer over low heat for 1 hour. Drain off the water and purée the hot lentils and vegetables in the blender, adding the chicken broth, butter, and cumin or curry powder.

Spread the lentils into a small buttered baking dish. Place the pork slices or chops on top of the purée and cover with aluminum foil. Heat in a preheated 350° oven for 25 minutes until the pork is hot.

Serve with a brown sauce.

COMMENT: When you are making a sauce for a roast, double the recipe and, if freezer space permits, freeze half the sauce in a small zip-lock bag. These bags lie flat and may be stacked one on top of another like the pages of a book and take up very little space. The frozen sauce can be put directly in a pan and reheated.

BROWN SAUCE

A simple white sauce is made by heating 1 tablespoon of butter, stir-
ring 1 tablespoon of flour into the butter, and adding 1 cup of milk or
chicken broth. The sauce is then seasoned with salt and pepper and per-
haps an herb. A brown sauce can be made in almost the same way, but
the butter and flour are heated until lightly browned and beef broth is
used to replace the chicken broth. However, to make a brown sauce of
greater depth and with a fuller richer flavor use the recipe below.

FOR 2 CUPS

2 tablespoons butter	1 bay leaf
1 onion, finely chopped	½ teaspoon thyme
1 carrot, finely chopped	3 sprigs parsley
1 stalk celery, finely chopped	1 teaspoon peppercorns
4 mushrooms, finely chopped	½ teaspoon salt
3 tablespoons flour	2 teaspoons tomato paste
4 cups homemade beef broth	2 tablespoons Madeira (optional)

Heat the butter and fry the onion, carrot, celery, and mushrooms for
5 minutes over moderate heat. Stir in the flour and cook for 2 minutes.
Add all the remaining ingredients except the Madeira. Simmer the sauce
uncovered for 2 hours until the quantity has reduced to 2 cups. Stir in
the Madeira.

COMMENT: This is a classic brown sauce and can be left simmering on
the stove while you go about your life's work. It does not require constant
attention. The sauce can be frozen, so it is worth making a reasonably
large amount at one time. Herbs such as ½ teaspoon tarragon or thyme
may be added and at the last moment a tablespoon of butter may be added
to enrich the sauce and make it shine.

THANKSGIVING DINNER

After the arguments, sometimes known as discussions, and the long distance phone calls have run their course, it may be decided that the place to spend Thanksgiving dinner is in the new household. The unstated aim will be to keep everybody happy, or at least equally unhappy.

At this point it is wise to establish some ground rules. When two people who live together also cook together, the results are either extraordinarily good or catastrophically terrible. Rarely is there any middle ground, and if there is, it is the lawyers that find it. So eliminate any potential sources of conflict in the beginning. Rather than trying to duplicate a specialty of another house, make up your mind to establish your own individual Thanksgiving dinner, or assign the giblet gravy, creamed onions, or pumpkin pie to the person who is the unchallenged expert.

In the free time of the week before Thanksgiving clean the apartment, the silver, the kitchen cupboards, and everything that may be open to inspection. Buy the food and start preparing it at least a day in advance so there will not be a frantic rush at the end.

Now you are ready to get down to the serious business of making the biggest and most elaborate meal of the year. If one person has decided that he or she is a cook of superior ability, then the other would be wise to accept the role of helper with as much willing enthusiasm as seems appropriate. The helper may offer to buy and unpack the groceries, wash the vegetables, and set the table. Part of the job also entails offering murmurings of support and occasional gasps of wonderment. Between these encouraging assertions, the helper could be usefully employed by washing the kitchen floor. (Two people in the kitchen make the floor six times dirtier than one person. Possibly there is a law of time and motion to explain why this is so.) The helper is not required to offer any gratuitous comments concerning the menu, which was agreed upon days ago; the state of the family budget; or the family as it is presently constituted, nor should the helper ruminate audibly whether it would have been better to have gone to somebody else's home for dinner. Having acquired all the rotten jobs in the kitchen, the helper may be entitled to feeling disgruntled, but in the end, when dinner is served triumphantly, it will all be worth the effort. The helper should be encouraged by the cook, who must remember to maintain a continuous and cheerful stream of witty remarks and offer the helper an occasional taste or drink to keep the spirits up.

The cook, who has the best of the bargain, is allowed to get a little tired but must not become harassed, irritable, or impatient, or everything will fall apart.

Of course none of these cautionary remarks may have any place in your kitchen, where the ambiance is sublime and the understanding total.

Thanksgiving dinner is really not a difficult meal to make, but to create the traditional feast does involve the making of several dishes. As with all elaborate meals, it is enormously helpful to make a list, not only of the dishes themselves, but also of the procedures that go into the making of the dish. Once everything has been written down, you will have a clearer idea of the length of time everything will take and, perhaps of equal importance, it is increasingly encouraging to see the list becoming shorter as the various steps are completed and crossed off.

THANKSGIVING DINNER MENU

Roast Stuffed Turkey	Giblet Gravy
Cranberry Sauce	
Baked Acorn Squash	Onions in Cream Sauce
Oysters on the Half Shell	
Baked Potatoes	Sweet Potato Casserole
Pumpkin Pie	Mincemeat Pie

———◆—

MAY BE DIVIDED ROUGHLY EQUALLY

Person A
Roast Turkey
Onions in Cream Sauce
Baked Potatoes
Pastry for 2 Pies
Complete Mincemeat Pie

Person B
Giblet Gravy
Baked Acorn Squash
Cranberry Sauce
Sweet Potato Casserole
Filling for Pumpkin Pie

❧ THANKSGIVING DINNER ❧
SHOPPING LIST

Meat and Fish
14-pound turkey
1 pound pork sausage meat
3 dozen (or more) oysters on the half shell

Vegetables and Fruit
3 yellow onions
2 pounds small white onions
Carrots
Celery
3 acorn squash
4 baking potatoes
4 medium-sized sweet potatoes
Parsley
Watercress
1 pound cranberries
1 orange
1 lemon

Dairy
1 pound butter
2 eggs
1 quart milk or more for children's drinks
3 (½ pint) cartons whipping cream

Grocery
2 cups chopped pecans
4 cups breadcrumbs
Salt
Pepper
Sugar
All-purpose flour
1-pound jar applesauce
Maple syrup
Brown sugar
1-pound can Crisco
2-pound can pumpkin pie filling
2 pounds mincemeat

Herbs and Spices
Sage
Thyme
Bay leaf
Paprika
Powdered ginger
Nutmeg
Cinnamon

Drinks
Wine
Cider
Milk
Tea
Coffee
Bourbon (optional)

ROAST STUFFED TURKEY

It is still possible to order a fresh rather than a frozen turkey in some places. If you can find one, the effort of searching will be rewarded.   FOR 12

Preheat oven to 350°.

14-pound turkey	1½ teaspoons salt
3 tablespoons butter	Freshly ground black pepper
2 onions, finely chopped	½ cup chopped parsley
2 stalks celery with the leaves,	1 teaspoon sage
finely chopped	1 teaspoon thyme
2 cups chopped pecans	2 eggs, lightly beaten
1 pound sausage meat	3 tablespoons solid shortening
4 cups freshly made breadcrumbs	1 teaspoon paprika

Remove the giblets from the turkey. Reserve the liver. (The remaining giblets will be used for giblet gravy.)

Heat the butter in a large frying pan. Add the onions and celery with the leaves and fry for 5 minutes. Add and fry the nuts for 5 minutes until lightly browned. Transfer these ingredients to a large mixing bowl. Add the turkey liver to the same butter and fry for 5 minutes. Remove and chop the liver. Add to the onions and celery.

Break up the sausage meat and fry for 10 minutes until all the fat has been rendered. Drain the sausage and place in the bowl. Stir in the breadcrumbs, 1 teaspoon of salt, pepper, parsley, sage, thyme, and eggs. Mix until well combined. Fill the dressing into the turkey cavity and truss with string or secure with poultry skewers.

Place the turkey on a rack in a roasting pan and rub the skin with shortening. Season with remaining salt and pepper and dust with paprika. Roast the turkey in a preheated oven for 4 hours. Test the turkey after 3½ hours by inserting the point of a sharp paring knife into the thigh. If the juice runs clear, without any trace of blood, and if the thigh moves easily in the joint, the turkey is done.

Remove from the oven and cover the turkey with foil. Leave it to rest for 30 minutes before carving.

COMMENT: After the turkey is taken from the oven it will continue to cook for at least 10 minutes as a result of its own internal heat. Be very careful not to overcook it or it will be dry and tasteless.

NOTE: The dressing may be made in advance and filled into the turkey cavity just before roasting.

TURKEY GIBLET GRAVY

This is essentially the same as the giblet gravy for roast chicken (see Index), but some of the ingredients have been increased.   FOR 12

Turkey giblets except the liver	½ teaspoon thyme
1 onion, finely chopped	1 teaspoon peppercorns
1 stalk celery, sliced	3 tablespoons butter
2 carrots, finely chopped	4 tablespoons flour
5 cups chicken broth	½ teaspoon salt
3 sprigs parsley	Freshly ground black pepper
1 bay leaf	

Place the giblets, onion, celery, carrots, chicken broth, parsley, bay leaf, thyme, and peppercorns in a saucepan. Simmer partially covered for 2 hours until the broth has reduced to 4 cups. Strain the broth.

Heat the butter in a clean saucepan. Stir in the flour and add the strained broth gradually to form a smooth gravy. Season with salt and pepper.

COMMENT: The gravy can be made in advance and reheated.

BAKED ACORN SQUASH

FOR 6 ON ANOTHER OCCASION
FOR 12 FOR THANKSGIVING

Preheat oven to 350°.

3 acorn squash	3 tablespoons maple syrup
3 tablespoons butter	1½ teaspoons powdered ginger
¾ cup applesauce	1 bunch watercress

Cut each squash in half through the center. Cut a slice from the base of each half so it will stand straight without tipping. Divide the remaining ingredients among the squash halves. Place in 2 large baking dishes filled to a depth of 1½″ with hot water. Cover with foil and bake in a preheated oven for 40 minutes. Remove the foil, drain off the water, and decorate the dish with watercress.

COMMENT: Even if you think you do not like squash, you will surely like it this way.

ONIONS IN CREAM SAUCE

When the table is groaning with so many good things to eat, do not make every dish to serve 12 people, as they will eat only a little of this and a little of that.

FOR 6 ON ANOTHER OCCASION
FOR 12 FOR THANKSGIVING

2 pounds small white onions, peeled	½ cup whipping cream
3 tablespoons butter	½ teaspoon salt
1 teaspoon sugar	Freshly ground black pepper
2 tablespoons flour	¼ teaspoon nutmeg
1¼ cups milk	1 teaspoon lemon juice
	2 tablespoons finely chopped parsley

Cut a cross in the root end of each onion to prevent the center from falling out of the onions. Simmer the onions in boiling salted water for 10 minutes. Drain the onions.

Heat the butter in a saucepan. Add the onions and sprinkle with sugar. Cook over low heat for 5 minutes until the onions are lightly browned. Stir in the flour and add the milk gradually to form a smooth sauce. Add the cream, salt, pepper, nutmeg, and lemon juice. Simmer for 10 minutes and garnish with parsley.

COMMENT: This dish can be made in advance and reheated. Add a little more milk if the sauce becomes too thick.

CRANBERRY SAUCE

Homemade cranberry sauce tastes infinitely better than the commercial variety.   FOR 12

1 pound (4 cups) cranberries	2 cups sugar
2 cups water	Grated rind of 1 orange

Wash the cranberries in a colander and discard any under- or over-ripe berries.

Pour the water into a saucepan and add the sugar. Stir over moderate heat until the sugar has dissolved. Boil the syrup for 10 minutes. Add the cranberries and simmer for 5 minutes. Remove from the heat and stir in the grated orange rind. Chill for 4 hours before serving.

COMMENT: The cranberry sauce will thicken as it cools. There will be some sauce left over, but as cranberries are always, it seems, packed in 1-pound boxes, this is unavoidable. The solution to the problem is to make a cranberry pie. Make the pastry for Mincemeat Pie (see index) and for the filling place the leftover cranberry sauce in a bowl, add 1 cup raisins soaked in boiling water for 5 minutes and drained, and 1 cup chopped pecans or other nuts. Sliced apples may also be added to make a quantity of 4 cups of filling. Stir in 2 tablespoons cornstarch dissolved in 3 tablespoons cold water to thicken the filling and enable the pie to be sliced easily. Flavor the filling with a touch of nutmeg (¼ teaspoon) and cinnamon (½ teaspoon), add a tablespoon of butter, and you will not only have a great pie for 6 people but will have solved the problem of the leftover cranberry sauce neatly. As for the leftover pie . . .

OYSTERS ON THE HALF SHELL

Oysters on the half shell need only to be arranged on a plate and garnished with lemon wedges. Slip them down between bites of other delectable deliciousnesses.

SWEET POTATO CASSEROLE

A Southern recipe for sweet potatoes that will surely become a specialty of the house.   FOR 6 ON ANOTHER OCCASION
FOR 12 FOR THANKSGIVING

Preheat oven to 350°.

4 medium-sized sweet potatoes	⅛ teaspoon nutmeg
¾ cup milk or light cream	¼ teaspoon cinnamon
2 tablespoons butter	½ cup applesauce
½ teaspoon salt	¼ cup brown sugar
Freshly ground black pepper	¼ cup Bourbon (optional)

Boil the sweet potatoes unpeeled in a large pan of salted water for 45 minutes until tender. Slip off the skins and mash the potatoes, adding sufficient milk or cream to soften. Add all the remaining ingredients and transfer to a buttered baking dish or casserole. Cover with aluminum foil and bake in a preheated oven for 30 minutes.

MINCEMEAT PIE

The pastry for this pie, the same as that used for Quiche Lorraine (see Index), can be used for making many other pies. For recipes for peach, blueberry, and other pies see Index.

FOR A DOUBLE CRUST 9″ PIE FOR 8 PEOPLE

Preheat oven to 350°.

2½ cups sifted all-purpose flour
¼ teaspoon salt
6 tablespoons butter, cut into small pieces

6 tablespoons solid shortening
9 tablespoons water
1 pound 12 ounce jar mincemeat

GLAZE

1 egg yolk combined with
1 tablespoon milk

Powdered sugar
Whipping cream

Place the flour and salt in a bowl. Add the butter and blend into the flour with the fingertips or a pastry blender until the butter is the size of small peas. Blend in the shortening in the same way. Stir in the water with a fork, adding a little at a time, until the dough can be formed into a ball. Wrap the ball in wax paper and chill in the refrigerator for 20 minutes.

Cut the ball of dough into unequal halves. Roll the larger half on a floured board with a floured rolling pin and fit into a 9″ pie plate. Add the mincemeat, mounding it up in the center.

Roll out the top crust and fit and trim the edges of the pastry over the mincemeat. Cut the design of a tree or a branch or whatever takes your fancy into the top crust, using a sharp knife. The cuts in pastry will permit steam to escape and keep the pastry crisp.

For the glaze, brush the top crust with 1 egg yolk combined with 1 tablespoon of milk to make a glossy golden crust.

Bake in a preheated oven for 40 minutes. Dust with powdered sugar and serve warm with large dollops of whipped cream.

PUMPKIN PIE

Make half the recipe for Mincemeat Pie (see Index) and fill with canned pumpkin pie filling. Bake according to the directions on the can.

OTHER FRUIT PIES:

Preheat oven to 350°.

APPLE PIE

Pastry for Mincemeat Pie (see Index)
4 large cooking apples, peeled,
    cored, and thinly sliced
½ cup sugar
¼ teaspoon nutmeg
½ teaspoon cinnamon
½ cup apricot preserves (optional)

2 tablespoons dark Jamaica rum
    (optional)
2 tablespoons cornstarch dissolved
    in 2 tablespoons cold water
2 tablespoons butter
Powdered sugar
Whipping cream

On the bottom crust place the apples, sugar, nutmeg, and cinnamon. Add the remaining ingredients. Cover with the top crust, cut slits in the top crust and bake in a preheated oven for 40 minutes. Dust with sifted powdered sugar and serve with whipped cream.

BLUEBERRY PIE

Pastry for Mincemeat Pie (see Index)
4 cups blueberries
½ cup red currant jelly

2 tablespoons cornstarch dissolved
    in 2 tablespoons cold water

Follow the directions for Apple Pie (given above).

Now that you have the idea, follow the same pattern to make:

PEACH PIE

4 cups diced peaches, skins removed
½ cup sugar
1 teaspoon cinnamon

2 tablespoons cornstarch dissolved
    in 2 tablespoons cold water

MIXED FRUIT PIE

4 cups total combined strawberries,
    blackberries, blueberries, sliced
    apples, or other fresh fruit

½ cup sugar
2 tablespoons cornstarch dissolved
    in 2 tablespoons cold water

It is an undisputable fact of life that no pie tastes good without whipped cream. Though some people may reject the idea, it will be for caloric rather than aesthetic reasons.

SPECIALTIES OF THE HOUSE

☙ PICNICS ☜

There are some picnics that are eaten at a desk, sitting on the floor of a new and empty apartment, or on a long car journey. Then there are other savored, relished, and remembered picnics on boats, back-pack picnics, picnics beside a still lake, beneath shady trees, or on summer beaches. Picnics are made from ham and cheese on rye or ambrosia and nectar. But whether they erupt spontaneously or are planned with the utmost care, the best picnics are those made with the freshest of foods.

A good deal of thought and planning goes into making a movable feast, and the best way to start is to make a list of all the things you will need. Leaving the food to one side for a moment, there are some basics that are constant and will be needed for almost every picnic. If you are very efficient and have many picnics, it is a good idea to keep all these odds and ends together inside the picnic hamper. If you are a dedicated lover of the outdoors, invest in some really beautiful picnic gear. Buy a handsome basket and colorful lightweight melamine dishes and utensils. The small amount of extra weight is worth carrying, for even the most Lucullan of delights will pale if it is allowed to ooze onto thirsty, floppy paper plates. Delicate glasses will not break if they are handled with care and wrapped in cloth napkins, for no wine can begin to taste good from a paper cup, and plastic does not weigh significantly less than glass, even though you say that plastic will not break. (The glasses are optional.)

If you are taking a wicker picnic basket to the beach, line it with foil and then a colorful cloth to keep the sand on the beach and not in your sandwich. Take along another tablecloth for spreading, and napkins, too.

Keep a corkscrew, a bottle and a can opener in the picnic basket along with a sharp knife and a lightweight cutting board. The Lucite or clear plastic boards weigh almost nothing, and it is helpful to have a firm surface for slicing sausage and other meats, vegetables, cheese, and bread. Miniature salt and pepper shakers are easily tucked into corners of the basket.

When packing the hamper, organize it in such a way that the foods that will be eaten first are on the top. If food is hidden beneath its wrappings, label each package separately. This will save a goodly amount of exploration. Empty peanut butter jars, coffee cans, and plastic boxes make good containers for soft foods, tomatoes, salad ingredients, butter, cheese, and berries. Tape the lids onto paper containers because they can easily become separated with disastrous results.

Many sandwiches taste fresher and better if they are put together at the picnic site, but if they are made in advance assemble them at the last minute and wrap each one, and other individual portions of foods, separately. Pick up fresh fruit at the last minute when it is practical.

Take the food out of the hamper as it is needed rather than leaving fruits, cheese, and desserts in the sun. Remember to put the hamper in the shade if possible to protect the uneaten food.

Homemade lemonade or iced tea is more refreshing than sweet carbonated drinks. Ice cubes can be made at home and stored in milk cartons. Hot coffee travels fairly well on a short journey but tends to become bitter when it has been made more than two hours in advance. It is surprisingly better to take some boiling water in a thermos flask and make instant coffee as you need it.

A few paper towels are handy for wiping off the plates, and a plastic garbage bag is often essential for the final cleanup. Take along a damp face towel in a plastic bag or the packaged lemon scented hand towels for freshening yourself. An insect repellent or, if it is already too late for prevention, a spray for coping with insect bites can make your time outside happier.

When you decide to cook over an open wood fire, take along a set of nesting utensils purchased from a camping store. Rub the outside of the pans with soap and they will be easier to clean. Use aluminum foil for lids. Remember to take a spoon for stirring and serving, a large fork for turning meats, and kitchen tongs. (A forked twig can be used if you forget the tongs.) An oven mitt may feel out of place but is very useful when you are wearing only a bathing suit and the pot is boiling over.

Take freeze-dried meats, vegetables, and eggs on overnight camping trips. They can be ordered by mail, and if you do not know where to write, pick up a copy of a camping magazine and find an address. Freeze-dried foods are easy to prepare and light to carry. Reconstitute dried milk as it is needed. Margarine in a plastic box is easier to carry than butter (life often hinges on small compromises). In fact, for camping trips take as many convenience foods as possible or you will find yourself spending all day in the "kitchen." Pancake and muffin, quick bread and cake mixes taste marvelous by moonlight, and instant rice, dried soups, instant coffee, and fruit juice concentrates are ready to eat, if not in an instant, at least very quickly.

On a boat the greatest difficulty is in keeping everything dry. Ziplock bags are particularly useful as they will not let moisture in or out and take up very little space. If the boat is small and the voyage long, it is a great comfort to have some hot food or a flask of hot soup or coffee. A tot of rum never did significant harm to anyone and certainly helps to keep the spirits up. Wrap hot casseroles in several layers of newspaper and then in an insulated waterproof bag to keep warm. If you have a stove on board, keep wooden matches in a screw-top glass jar or a plastic bag, and if you happen to catch a passing fish, keep it in a pail of water until you are ready to cook it. When you are docked put a stone in the pail. Cover the stone with leaves as a bed for the fish and cover the fish with a layer of leaves. Sink the weighted pail at the water's edge. Arrange some large stones around the pail to prevent it from tipping and remind yourself to notice if you are in tidal waters.

PICNIC SNACKS

It is an extraordinary fact that the view of the highest mountain, the clearest lake, or the vastest ocean is brought into sharper focus when you have something to eat readily at hand.

Sprinkle sliced avocado with salt and lemon juice

Dip radishes in softened butter and sprinkle with salt

Put tiny new hot boiled potatoes in foil, add a knob of butter and chopped chives

Cubes of Cheddar cheese and English walnuts

Cubes of salami dipped in German mustard

Cubes of melon and prosciutto ham secured with toothpicks

Cubes of ham and black olives

Cherry tomatoes stuffed with combined Roquefort and cream cheeses

Celery and carrot sticks, of course

Stuffed eggs

Dried apricots

Chocolate, raisins, and almonds

Apples and homemade cookies

SANDWICH IDEAS

If you have grown weary of ham and Swiss on rye, you may enjoy one of the following sandwiches.

Cut crisp Italian rolls or French bread in half. Scoop out most of the center and fill with:

Layers of salami, ham, smoked sausage, cheese slices, and roasted peppers, sprinkle with oregano and olive oil

Cold scrambled eggs and diced boiled ham

Steak tartare (see Index)

Chicken salad

Tuna salad

Shrimp salad

Smoked salmon and cream cheese

Reassemble the rolls.

Use whole grain, cracked wheat, pumpernickel, rye, or other bread to make:

Egg and watercress sandwiches

Chicken and ham sandwiches with mustard-flavored mayonnaise

Corned beef and mustard-flavored mayonnaise

Chicken liver pâté and sliced apple

Salmon and cucumber

Sardines, lemon juice, and lettuce

Cold sausage and mustard

Cold turkey and dressing

Cream cheese, grated orange rind, and chopped walnuts

Cream cheese and canned pesto

Cream cheese, avocado slices, and bean sprouts

Cream cheese and crumbled cooked bacon

Roquefort cheese and sliced pears

Camembert cheese and sliced apples

Cheddar cheese and chutney

CHICKEN TURNOVERS

Chicken-filled pastries are a good alternative to a sandwich. They can be picked up and eaten with your fingers.   FOR 6

Preheat oven to 375°.

Pastry for Quiche Lorraine (see Index)	**2 tablespoons butter**
1½ cups cooked chicken	**1 onion, finely chopped**
1 cup diced boiled potatoes	**¼ teaspoon salt**
½ cup peas and carrots, cooked	**Freshly ground black pepper**

G L A Z E

**1 egg yolk combined with
1 tablespoon milk**

Prepare the pastry.

Combine the chicken, potatoes, and vegetables in a bowl. Heat the butter and fry the onion for 3 minutes. Add to the ingredients in the bowl. Season the mixture with salt and pepper.

Roll the pastry on a floured counter and cut into 6 (7") circles. Brush the edges of the pastry with cold water. Place part of the mixture in the middle of each circle. Lift up the edges of the pastry over the filling and pinch the sides together to enclose it completely. Place the pastries on a buttered and floured baking sheet and brush with egg yolk combined with milk. Bake in a preheated oven for 35 minutes and serve the pastries hot or cold.

COMMENT: Pastry can be made in advance and frozen either cooked or uncooked. To make a quick pastry shell, use frozen puff pastry shells. Thaw the pastry in the refrigerator and knead for a minute or two before rolling.

SCOTCH EGGS

Scotch eggs are a great idea for picnics. The sausage meat is wrapped around a hard-cooked egg and the whole thing is deep-fried until it is slightly browned and crisp. You can eat a Scotch egg in your hand or serve it on a lettuce leaf with a little mustard on the side.   FOR 2

2 hard-cooked eggs	**Shortening for deep frying**
¼ cup flour for dredging	**Mustard for dipping**
½ cup pork sausage meat	

Dredge the eggs in flour. Form the sausage meat into 2 patties, flattening it between the palms of your hands. Wrap the egg in sausage meat, making sure it is completely enclosed. Dredge in flour again.

Heat the shortening to 375° and fry the Scotch eggs for 4 minutes. Drain and serve hot or cold with mustard.

COMMENT: Though this appears to be a very brief time for frying the sausage meat, do not worry, it will be completely cooked.

MEDITERRANEAN POTATO SALAD

A colorful salad full of good strong flavors that make a great accompaniment for cold chicken.   FOR 2

4 cold boiled potatoes, peeled	1 tablespoon finely chopped chives
⅓ cup mayonnaise	1 tomato, chopped
2 tablespoons sour cream	4 black olives, pitted and chopped
2 anchovy fillets, chopped	1 tablespoon chopped pimiento
½ teaspoon capers	

Slice the potatoes and place in a bowl. Stir together the mayonnaise and sour cream. Fold in all the remaining ingredients.

COMMENT: Potatoes can be peeled and stored in the refrigerator in a bowl of salted water for 24 hours. Do not cook potatoes for potato salad beyond the point when they can be pierced easily with a sharp knife.

MAYONNAISE

Homemade mayonnaise is easy to make and elevates a simple salad into a memorable meal.   MAKES 2 CUPS

2 egg yolks	1 tablespoon finely chopped parsley
¼ teaspoon salt	(optional)
¼ teaspoon mild Dijon mustard	2 teaspoons finely chopped chives
1 tablespoon lemon juice	(optional)
¾ cup vegetable oil	½ teaspoon tarragon (optional)
¾ cup olive oil	

Place the egg yolks, salt, mustard, and lemon juice in a bowl and beat at high speed with an electric beater for 3 minutes until the egg yolks have thickened. Add the combined oils very, very slowly (barely a drop at a time) until ½ cup of oil has been added. Continue adding the oil at a slightly faster rate until it is all used while continuing to beat constantly. Taste the mayonnaise and add more salt or lemon juice if necessary. Beat in the herbs.

SAUSAGES IN PASTRY

A simple sausage is a splendid feast when it is wrapped in a blanket of pastry.   FOR 4

Preheat oven to 350°.

8 sausages (bratwurst, knackwurst, or other firm sausage)	4 or more teaspoons German mustard

PASTRY

¾ cup sifted flour	1 tablespoon solid shortening
¼ teaspoon salt	2 or 3 tablespoons cold water
2 tablespoons butter	

GLAZE

1 egg yolk combined with
1 tablespoon milk

Cook the sausages for 5 minutes and remove the skins if necessary. Spread the sausages with mustard.

To prepare the pastry, put the flour and salt in a bowl. Cut the butter into small pieces. Add the shortening and mix the ingredients with the fingertips or a pastry blender until the butter is the size of small peas. Stir in the water with a fork and form the mixture into a ball. Wrap the ball in wax paper and chill in the refrigerator for 20 minutes. Roll the pastry on a floured board and cut into 8 equal parts.

Brush the edges of the pastry with cold water so it will seal itself. Roll the sausages in pastry and place on a buttered and floured baking sheet. Brush with egg yolk combined with milk and bake in a preheated oven for 40 minutes until the pastry is golden brown. Serve hot or cold.

COMMENT: The egg and milk glaze is used on all surface crust pastry recipes such as apple and blueberry pies. It is brushed on many breads before they are baked. The glaze gives a beautiful color and professional finish to these preparations.

MARINATED CUCUMBERS

Marinated cucumbers make an interesting change from the customary side dish salads and are particularly enjoyable with cold striped bass or other cold poached fish.   FOR 4

1 cucumber, peeled and thinly sliced
4 paper-thin slices peeled onion
2 teaspoons salt
1 tablespoon lemon juice

½ cup sour cream
1 teaspoon finely chopped fresh
    mint or ½ teaspoon dillweed

Place the cucumber slices in a bowl. Add the onion, salt, and lemon juice. Toss to combine the ingredients. Cover with a plate and place a 1-pound food can on the plate to weight it. Chill in the refrigerator for 1 hour. Pour off the liquid that forms and pat the cucumber slices dry on paper towels. Stir in the sour cream and mint or dillweed.

COMMENT: As the excess water is pressed from the cucumber, the slices become firm and crisp.

BREAD

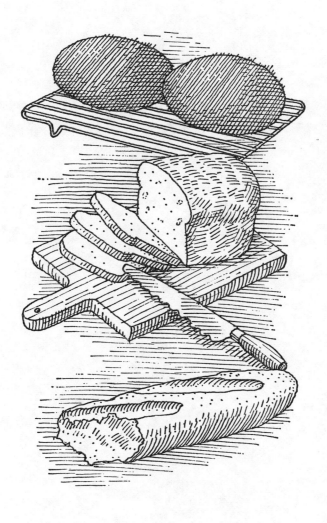

✤ BREAD ✥

Bread is one of the most satisfying of all foods to make, to eat, and to share. More and more people are making their own bread, searching out health food stores and little specialty food stores to find whole grain, cracked grain, and rye flours. The results of bread making are usually good, for little can go seriously wrong with them. If you are armed with a few facts, your bread can and will be spectacularly good. These are the things to know.

Yeast Yeast is a living organism that begins to work in the presence of moisture. It is like a seed that comes to life when it is planted. The ideal conditions for growth are a medium of milk or water at a temperature of 105°–15°. This is slightly above body temperature, a cool lukewarm. If the yeast is put into a liquid below this temperature, it will work but slowly and reluctantly. If, however, the temperature is too high, the yeast is shocked and killed. It turns itself off like an electric light and is totally, irretrievably dead.

If the yeast is active, it will soften in the liquid, making it cloudy, and will create a slight bubbling effect as gas is released. If there is no action, either the liquid was too hot or the yeast was too old. Be sure to check the expiration date on the package.

Sugar increases the action of the yeast, and salt slows it down. Both sugar and salt are added to almost all yeast doughs. Too much sugar will cause the bread to rise too rapidly, creating air pockets, and too large a quantity of salt will inhibit the action of the yeast, making a dense and poorly risen bread.

Fresh, or compressed, yeast is grayish white in color and crumbly in texture. It can be stored for up to two weeks in the refrigerator in a jar with a tightly fitting lid, or it can be frozen for two months. Frozen yeast should be thawed at room temperature and used immediately. One ½-ounce package of fresh yeast can be substituted for 1 package (1 tablespoon) of active dry yeast.

Baking powder is used instead of yeast for making quick breads such as biscuits and corn bread. Baking soda is sometimes added to breads containing fruits that are high in acid to neutralize their effect.

Flour Bread flour is a so-called "hard" flour, high in gluten. This virtue enables the flour to absorb more liquid and retain the gasses produced by the yeast. In turn the dough itself will have a greater elasticity when it is kneaded, and the bread will rise better and have a finer crumb and crust than bread made with "soft" or all-purpose flour. Kneading helps to develop the gluten in the flour.

All-purpose flour is blended from hard and soft wheat, and the proportions vary throughout the country.

Cake flour and pastry flour are made from soft wheat and are not recommended for breadmaking. The bread does not rise well and is difficult to slice. Bread made with these flours lacks both taste and body.

Whole wheat flour and graham flour are both high in gluten. They are excellent for breadmaking and contain all the natural vitamins and minerals. These flours require very little kneading and produce a firm, well-textured bread. Whole wheat and graham flours can be used to replace all or part of the quantity of plain bread flour in any recipe.

Enriched flour has had the wheat grain removed to extend its shelf life. The nutrients that are removed are then replaced with synthetics, which, though they are not in any way harmful and may even be good for your health, do not produce as good-tasting a loaf of bread as the natural flours.

⋈ HOW TO MAKE BREAD ⋉

STEP 1:　Sponge

Fresh or dry yeast is sprinkled onto lukewarm water or milk. Water makes a coarse "French bread" type of crumb and milk gives a soft crumb. Except in the making of French and Italian breads, sugar or honey is added to "feed" the yeast and salt is added to control the action of the yeast. Oil or butter may be added to enrich and soften the dough and the crumb. The yeast mixture is combined with a minimum quantity of flour to form a soft dough. The dough is kneaded, and sufficient flour is added until the dough is soft and elastic and no longer sticky.

STEP 2:　Rising

The dough is placed in a buttered large bowl. The surface is brushed with butter to prevent it from becoming dry and is then covered with a cloth to exclude any possible drafts. The dough is left to rise until it has doubled in size. This will take from 1 to 4 hours, depending on the type of dough.

STEP 3:　Proving

The dough is punched down in the bowl and kneaded again for two or three minutes. It is then shaped into loaves or rolls and placed in buttered and floured loaf pans or on baking sheets. The dough is covered and left to rise for an hour until it has again doubled in bulk.

STEP 4: **Baking**
The dough may or may not be brushed with a glaze made from an egg yolk combined with milk, with beaten egg white, or with water. The top of the dough may be slashed with two or three cuts to make a more attractive appearance. The dough is baked in a preheated oven. It is ready when it begins to shrink from the sides of the pan. When it is tapped it emits a hollow empty sound. This last hollow laughter test is very difficult to perform, one can never be quite, quite sure. . . . However, if you stick closely to the time given in the recipe, you cannot go too far wrong.

NOTE ON STORING BREAD DOUGH

If you have to leave the kitchen for several hours, place the dough in the refrigerator. It will continue to rise but very slowly. You can bring it to room temperature, let the dough double in bulk, and bake it when you are ready.

Unbaked bread dough can also be frozen. It will spring back to life when it reaches room temperature.

Baked breads also freeze very successfully.

⚞ KNEADING ⚟

As the dough is kneaded it becomes firm and smooth, seeming to acquire strength within the body of the dough itself. Fold the dough toward you and press it down firmly and authoritatively with the heels of your hands. Turn it a quarter of circle. Turn and fold. Press and turn. Gradually a rhythm will develop. A rhythm that made all those legendary millers sing all those jolly songs that made such good bread. General Mills does not sing.

Gather more flour into the dough if it feels sticky, but do not add too much or the bread will be heavy. When you have the dough in front of you, you will get the "feel" of how much flour to add. When the dough has absorbed as much flour as it wants, it does not pick up anymore, so do not force it. When small air blisters appear beneath the surface of the dough and it is smooth and firm, let the dough, and yourself, rest. The dough will rise slowly, usually taking about two hours to double in bulk and form a smooth dome.

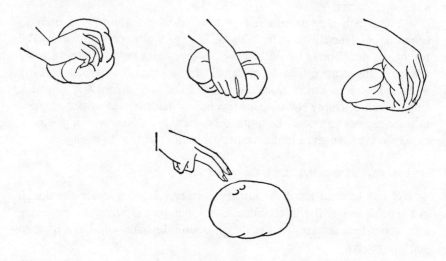

❧ WHITE BREAD AND VARIATIONS ☙

As you will see from the following recipes, all breads follow the same basic pattern. Either the total quantity of white flour is used or ½ the amount of white flour is replaced with whole wheat, rye, or graham flour. These flours all absorb more water than white flour, so, whereas white bread may take a little more than 5 cups, the other breads will take slightly less flour. The quantity of sugar may be varied up to ¼ cup according to your own taste, and the sugar may be substituted for honey in white breads, and molasses in date breads. Also the salt may be varied from 1 teaspoon to 1 tablespoon according to your taste, but do not add more than 1 tablespoon. As for the butter, it can be substituted for margarine or oil. The more butter that is added, the softer will be the crumb when the bread is sliced.

The variations of bread recipes are endless. Sour cream or cottage cheese can replace the milk and the milk can be replaced with water or beer. Herbs do not change the texture of the bread but improve the flavor. Add up to ½ cup finely chopped herbs or 1–2 tablespoons dried herbs to 5 cups of flour.

WHITE BREAD

This is an all-purpose bread for spreading with butter and preserves, for sandwiches and for toasting.   MAKES 2 LOAVES

1 package dry yeast
1 cup lukewarm water at 110°
1 cup milk
3 tablespoons butter

2 tablespoons sugar or honey
2 teaspoons salt
5 cups unbleached flour

GLAZE

1 egg yolk combined with
  1 tablespoon milk

Sprinkle the yeast over the water. Stir and leave to one side for 10 minutes. Heat the milk to simmering point. Cut the butter into small pieces and add to the milk. Add the sugar and salt and stir to dissolve. Leave to cool to 110°.

Pour the yeast and milk mixtures into a large bowl, add sufficient flour to form a dough (approximately 4 cups). Turn the dough onto the counter and knead for 5 minutes, adding more flour as necessary to prevent the dough from sticking to your hands and the counter. Continue kneading until the dough is smooth and firm. Small bubbles will appear beneath the surface and as the dough is kneaded the dough springs back on itself, expanding when pressure is applied and bouncing back when the pressure is released.

Place the dough in a buttered bowl, turning it over so that the entire surface is buttered. Cover with a kitchen towel and leave in a warm, draft-free spot in the kitchen for 2 hours until it doubles in size.

Punch the dough with your fist to release the gases. Cut the dough into 2 pieces. Knead again for 3 or 4 minutes and shape into 2 loaves to fit 9 x 5 x 3″ buttered loaf pans sprinkled with flour. The bread can also be made into round loaves or rolls and baked on prepared baking sheets. Cover the dough and leave for 1 hour until again doubled in bulk.

Preheat the oven to 375°. Brush the dough with 1 egg yolk combined with 1 tablespoon of milk. Bake the loaves for 45 minutes and rolls for 30 minutes. Remove the bread from the oven and leave in the pans for 5 minutes. If possible leave to cool on wire racks for at least an hour before slicing.

COMMENT: If you slice the bread too soon, it will be doughy and indigestible. Children love it this way.

To obtain a coarser crumb, use 2 cups of water instead of 1 cup of water and 1 cup of milk and reduce the butter to 1 tablespoon.

WHOLE WHEAT BREAD

Whole wheat bread is made in exactly the same way as white bread, but substitute half of the white flour for whole wheat flour.

RYE BREAD

Follow the directions for making white bread, substituting half of the white flour for rye flour. You will need slightly less than 5 cups of flour.

VARIATIONS

* Dark molasses may be used to replace the sugar or honey.

* 2 teaspoons of caraway, fennel, or dill seeds may also be added to the dough.

* Powdered milk may replace whole milk. (Dissolve 1 cup powdered milk in 1 cup of water. There will then be a total of 2 cups of water and 1 cup of powdered milk to replace 2 cups of liquid in white bread recipe.)

* 1 cup sour cream may be used to replace the milk.

OATMEAL BREAD

Yet another variation of white bread (see Index). Compare the recipes and see how similar they are.   MAKES 2 LOAVES

1 package dry yeast	2 cups white flour
2 cups lukewarm water at 110°	1½ cups rolled oats
3 tablespoons butter, melted	1½ cups whole wheat flour
2 tablespoons honey	(approximately)
2 teaspoons salt	

Sprinkle the yeast over the water. Stir and leave to one side for 10 minutes. Stir in the butter, honey, and salt. Pour into a large bowl and add the flour and oats. Add ½ cup whole wheat flour. Turn the dough onto the counter and knead the dough. Continue adding sufficient whole wheat flour until the dough sticks to neither your hands nor the counter but is smooth and firm. Continue with the directions for making white bread.

SAFFRON BREAD WITH RAISINS

Soak ½ teaspoon saffron filaments in ¼ cup boiling water for 5 minutes. Soak 1 cup raisins in 1 cup boiling water for 5 minutes. Drain the raisins and pat them dry on paper towels. Dredge the raisins in flour.

Follow the recipe for white bread (see Index) but sprinkle the yeast over ¾ cup lukewarm water. Stir and leave to one side for 10 minutes, add the saffron with the soaking water. Continue with the recipe, adding the dredged raisins to the dough after it has risen for the first time.

VARIATIONS

* Use ½ cup raisins and ½ cup chopped nuts. Dredge the nuts in flour to prevent them from sinking to the bottom of the bread.

* Substitute 1 cup raisins for 1 cup chopped glacéed fruit. Dredge the fruit in flour.

SPICED BREAD

Follow the directions for making white bread (see Index), but when the milk has cooled to 110° stir in 2 eggs, lightly beaten. Add to the flour 1 teaspoon cinnamon, ¼ teaspoon nutmeg, freshly grated if possible, and 1 teaspoon allspice. The grated rind of 2 oranges and 1 lemon may also be added. Dust the baked bread with sifted powdered sugar.

CHEDDAR CHEESE BREAD

Substitute 2 cups of beer for the water and milk in the recipe for white bread (see Index).

When the dough has risen for the first time, punch it down and knead into the dough 1 cup grated Cheddar cheese and ½ cup fresh dillweed or 1½ tablespoons dried dillweed.

* 1 onion, finely chopped and fried for 5 minutes in 2 tablespoons butter, may also be added to the dough at the same time as the cheese.

* ½ cup chopped walnuts dredged in flour may also be added to the bread at the same time as the cheese.

HOMEMADE PIZZA

The crust for this pizza is made with a yeast dough. It is not at all difficult to prepare. All the ingredients are mixed in a bowl, and then two hours later the pastry is rolled out. When it is baked it is light, crisp, and flaky and can be used for all manner of other pies, too.   FOR 4

½ package yeast	2 tablespoons butter
2 tablespoons lukewarm water	1 egg
1¼ cups flour	¼ cup cold water
¼ teaspoon salt	

Sprinkle the yeast over the lukewarm water. Stir once and leave to stand for 10 minutes. In the meantime, measure the flour and salt into a bowl. Cut the butter into small pieces and blend into the flour with the fingertips or a pastry blender until the pieces are the size of small peas. Stir the egg with the water and add to the flour mixture along with the yeast. Stir with a fork and form into a ball. Knead the pastry for a minute or two and place in a buttered clean bowl. Cover the bowl with a kitchen towel and leave for 2 hours until it has doubled in bulk. Roll the pastry into a 10″ circle and fit it into a flan ring or shallow tart tin.

TO MAKE THE FILLING:

Preheat oven to 350°.

3 tablespoons oil	½ teaspoon salt
2 onions, finely chopped	Freshly ground black pepper
2 cloves garlic, finely chopped	1 cup sliced Polish sausage
4 tomatoes, peeled, seeded, and chopped, or 1-pound can of tomatoes with their juice	1 cup grated Swiss or Gruyère cheese
1 tablespoon tomato paste	2-ounce can anchovy fillets, cut in half lengthwise
½ teaspoon oregano	12 black olives, pitted
½ teaspoon sugar	Freshly grated Parmesan cheese

Heat the oil and fry the onions and garlic for 5 minutes. Add the tomatoes, tomato paste, oregano, sugar, salt and pepper. Cook uncovered over low heat until almost all of the juice from the tomatoes has evaporated and the mixture has reduced to a thick purée. Spread the purée on top of the unbaked pastry shell. Scatter sausage slices and grated cheese on top of the purée and bake in a preheated oven for 30 minutes.

Decorate the pizza with a crisscross pattern of anchovies and with olives. Serve with a bowl of Parmesan cheese.

COMMENT: Many people seem anxious about making pastry and are even more concerned about working with yeast. Yet the preparation of the pastry is no more complicated than making a salad. Just follow the recipe, and after you have made it the first time, you will think nothing of pizza for twenty people.

SAUSAGE BREAD

Precook 12 pork sausages until all the fat has been rendered. When the white bread dough (see Index) has risen for the first time, punch the dough down. Pinch off pieces of dough and roll with a rolling pin to form a rectangle slightly larger than the sausage. Wrap each sausage in dough and pinch the edges together. Leave to rise for an hour. Brush the dough with the egg yolk and with glaze and bake in the preheated 375° oven for 30 minutes. Make a free-form loaf with the remaining dough.

Cooked sausage meat or leftover stuffing may also be distributed throughout the dough after the first rising, using your hands (there is no other way to do it).

These breads are very good to take on a picnic. Spread slices with butter flavored with mustard and eat them as they are, or use for turkey or other sandwiches.

GINGERBREAD

A fragrant warm bread to be served with tea or hot chocolate and a bowl of whipped cream. MAKES 9 SQUARES

Preheat oven to 350°.

2 eggs	Grated rind of 1 orange
1 cup sugar	2 teaspoons ginger
½ cup butter	1 teaspoon allspice
1 cup boiling water	1 teaspoon baking soda
¼ cup dark molasses	½ teaspoon baking powder
2 cups sifted flour	

Beat the eggs and sugar until very thick. Cut the butter into small pieces and add to the boiling water. Stir to dissolve the butter and add the molasses. Combine all the remaining ingredients. Fold the liquid and dry ingredients into the eggs and sugar alternately. Pour into a buttered 8 x 8 x 2" baking pan and bake in a preheated oven for 45 minutes or until a toothpick inserted into the center of the cake comes out clean. Leave the gingerbread to cool for 15 minutes before cutting.

QUICHE LORRAINE

⚜ MAKING PASTRY ⚜

Even if you cannot sing, dance, or recite a sonnet, you can make pastry. All you have to do is measure some flour and salt into a bowl, mix in some shortening, add water, and it is done. It is not a talent or a skill that requires years of training or divine inspiration; anybody can do it. After I have said that a few words of explanation follow.

Bread and pastry are man and wife. Both are created from the same basics but differ in certain particulars. The foundation of both bread and pastry is flour, salt, shortening, and water. When the ingredients are combined to form a dough, the two preparations become quite different. The difference lies in the handling of the dough. Bread dough is kneaded to develop the gluten in the flour, while pastry is handled as little as possible so that the gluten will not be developed. Gluten gives bread "body" but makes pastry tough. Bread dough thrives in a warm, moist oven, but pastry demands a cool room, cool hands, and a dry oven. Pastry should not be baked in the oven with a roast. The roast steams in the oven and will prevent pastry crust from becoming crisp.

The choice of one pastry recipe rather than another depends on the use to which it will be put. For instance, the pastry crust that surrounds a pâté or encases a whole fish, boneless ham, or filet of beef must be stronger than the pastry for a pie because the dough must be capable of absorbing juices from the food. The pastry for a fruit tart can, on the other hand, be as crisp as a cookie dough because it is used for an entirely different purpose.

Though the relationship of the flour to the shortening may be changed from one recipe to another and egg yolks may be substituted for water, the principles of making pastry remain the same. Too much flour will make the dough crumbly and very difficult to roll; it will be dry when it is baked. Too much shortening or water will also make the pastry difficult to roll, as it will be sticky. The pastry will not cook evenly and remain "doughy" even after an extended cooking time. It is important to measure the ingredients for pastry accurately.

Use a dry measuring cup for dry ingredients so the flour can be leveled precisely.

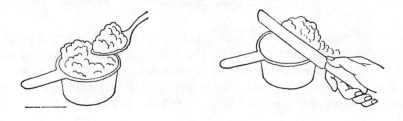

Leave the dough to "rest" for at least 20 minutes in the refrigerator so that the liquid will be dispersed evenly, before attempting to roll the pastry. If the dough is too cold when it is removed from the refrigerator, knead it very lightly for a minute or two until it is a soft malleable ball.

Roll the pastry on a lightly floured counter with a floured rolling pin. Roll it quickly and fit it well into the pie plate before trimming off the edges with a sharp knife. The pastry can be frozen either baked or unbaked.

When making a fruit tart or a pie with a large amount of liquid, it is best to bake the shell so it is partially "set" before adding the filling ingredients. This preliminary cooking is called "baking blind." However, you cannot bake the shell just as it is, or the pastry will slide down the sides of the pie plate, while the bottom will bubble into hills, valley and craters. To prevent this from happening, tear off a piece of foil slightly larger than the pie plate. Oil the foil and place it, oiled side down, on top of the pastry and fold the edges firmly over the sides of the plate to hold the pastry in place. Now, weight the foil with a single layer of dried beans and this will hold the bottom crust down. The beans can be used over and over again for the same purpose; they will not become rancid because they are dry.

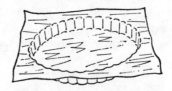

Bake the pastry in a preheated 375° oven for 10 minutes. Save the beans and discard the foil. Prick the bottom of the pastry to prevent air bubbles from becoming trapped and continue baking for 10 to 20 minutes, depending on the recipe and whether you want a fully baked empty pie shell, or, alternatively, add the filling ingredients at this point.

QUICHE LORRAINE

Quiche Lorraine is a flavored custard baked in a pastry shell. Quiche *is a French word meaning "tart," and this classic version was first made in Alsace-Lorraine.* FOR 6

Preheat oven to 375°.

PASTRY

1¼ cups sifted all-purpose flour	2 tablespoons shortening or
¼ teaspoon salt	margarine
4 tablespoons butter	4 tablespoons water

Sift the flour and salt together and place in a bowl. Cut the butter into small pieces and blend into the flour with the fingertips or a pastry blender. When the pieces are about the size of small peas, blend in the shortening or margarine. Stir in the water a little at a time with a fork. Add more water if necessary to form the mixture into a ball. (Different flours absorb varying quantities of water, so it is not possible to be exact in the water measurement.) Wrap the dough in a piece of wax paper and leave in the refrigerator for 20 minutes. Roll out the pastry and fit it into a 9″ pie plate. Cover the pastry with a piece of oiled foil, oiled side down, weight the foil with a single layer of dried beans, and bake in a preheated oven for 10 minutes. Remove the beans and foil and add the custard ingredients.

CUSTARD

4 eggs	2 tablespoons melted butter
¾ cup milk	½ teaspoon salt
¾ cup whipping cream	⅛ teaspoon cayenne pepper
1 tablespoon flour	⅛ teaspoon nutmeg
1 cup grated Swiss or Gruyère cheese	½ pound bacon fried until crisp and crumbled

Stir together all the custard ingredients. Sprinkle the cheese and bacon into the pie shell and pour in the custard slowly. Place in a preheated oven for 40 minutes until the custard is firm, puffy, and lightly browned. Serve warm or cold.

COMMENT: The quiche can be varied in many ways. Prepare the crust and the custard, keep the cheese, but leave out the bacon and add one of the following:

¾ cup cooked asparagus tips

¾ cup crab meat or other shellfish
2 teaspoons tomato paste and
1 tablespoon cocktail sherry

¾ cup sliced mushrooms, fried briefly in 2 tablespoons butter

¼ pound smoked salmon, cut into small pieces, and 4 chopped scallions simmered for 5 minutes in ¼ cup white vermouth

¾ cup sliced cooked Polish sausage and 2 teaspoons prepared mustard

10-ounce package frozen, cooked, and drained chopped spinach
¾ cup chopped tomatoes and ¼ cup diced boiled ham

As you can see, the possible combinations are limitless. Herbs may be added to the basic custard, and part of the liquid may be replaced with wine, if you fancy that on the palate of your imagination.

HOMEMADE JAMS AND JELLIES

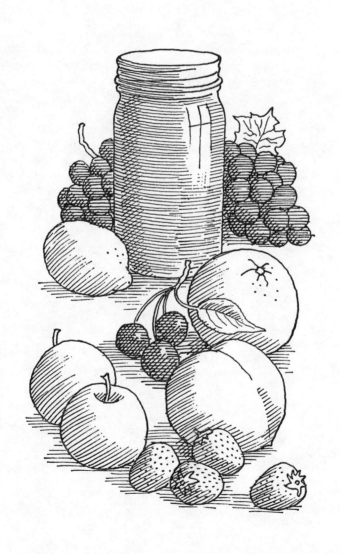

❧ HOMEMADE JAMS AND JELLIES ❧

When you plant a tree, paint a portrait, or write a book, it has a degree of permanence that a broiled fish or fruit pie can never hope to achieve. Perhaps this is why it is sometimes discouraging to spend many hours in the kitchen only to be left with a memory, a temporarily full and contented stomach, and a pile of dirty dishes.

The contrast is less obvious when food is preserved, canned, or pickled. In this case, you work all day, at the height of the summer heat, and there is nothing for dinner. However, you do have something. Rows and rows of beautiful jars of fruits, vegetables, jams, and jellies. Enough to last for a year of eating and spreading and a feeling of satisfaction and accomplishment that is hard to match.

❧ JAMS, PRESERVES, JELLIES, ❧ AND MARMALADE

Jam is made from crushed fruit and sugar. Almost all jams are made from a ratio of three cups of sugar to one quart of crushed fruit. The mixture is boiled until the temperature reaches 220°, packed into hot sterile jars, and sealed with liquid paraffin wax.

Preserves are made from whole berries or pieces of fruit, evenly distributed throughout a thick sugar syrup. Though preserves are used for spreading on bread or as an ice-cream topping, they are not as firm in consistency as jam.

Jellies are made from fruit juice and sugar. Pectin is added to some fruit juices so they will set.

Marmalade is made from chopped fruit and fruit rinds suspended in a clear jelly.

❧ PECTIN ❧

Pectin is the substance that causes jams and jellies to set. All fruits contain some pectin, though some, such as apples, contain more than others. Underripe fruit contains more pectin than fully ripened fruit. When the fruit is fully ripened, and for fruits naturally low in pectin, commercial pectin must be added (see specific recipes).

❧ SUGAR ❧

Sugar acts as a preservative for fruits. In solution it enters the cellular structure of the fruit, making it firm and maintaining the shape. Though honey can be substituted for the sugar, it does not produce such a clear color. Use only half the quantity of honey. Compared with sugar, honey is sweeter.

❧ BUYING THE FRUITS AND ❧ VEGETABLES FOR PRESERVES AND CANNING

The quality of homemade preserves is, of course, entirely dependent on the quality of the basic ingredients. It is tempting to buy a bushel basket of fruits and vegetables, but if you do, keep the following in mind:

1. It is best to use a portion of underripe rather than all ripe fruit and vegetables. Underripe fruit holds its shape, has a full fresh flavor, and contains a high proportion of pectin, which causes jams and jellies to set. When slightly underripe produce is cooked, the color becomes bright and clear.

2. Overripe produce has an unpleasant taste. When cooked, the color fades, and the texture softens.

3. The best results of canning and preserving are achieved by preparing the foods in small batches. It is infinitely better to buy and prepare small quantities of really fresh ingredients rather than to spend days on end to use up a depressingly large quantity of deteriorating fruits. Fruits

and tomatoes at the bottom of a large basket become damaged by the weight of fruits pressing on them. Unless you can have sufficient refrigerator space in which soft fruits such as berries, peaches, and tomatoes can be unpacked promptly and arranged in a single layer, you will run into the problem of filling the kitchen with fruit flies and squashed, rotting produce. In other words, think very carefully before investing in food bargains.

⊱ HOW TO MAKE JAM ⊰

1. Use a combination of fully ripe and slightly underripe fruit if possible. The underripe fruit contains natural pectin that will ensure that the jam will set.

2. Wash the fruit and discard any that is damaged. Cut away bruised part of otherwise perfect fruits. Crush berries and cut whole fruits such as plums into small pieces. Remove pits from cherries, and skins from peaches.

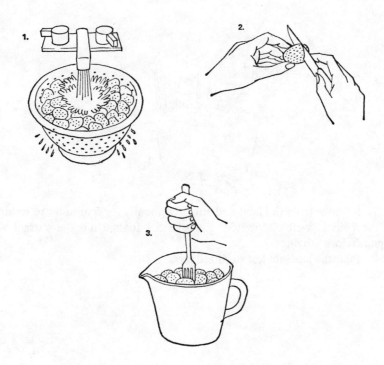

3. Measure the fruit in a glass measuring jar after it has been prepared.

4. Place the fruit in a heavy saucepan. Add 3 cups of sugar to every 4 cups of fruit.

5. Bring to boiling point, stirring occasionally until the sugar has dissolved in the fruit juice.

6. When the mixture reaches boiling point, boil it steadily until it reaches 220° on a candy thermometer.

7. Remove from the heat and stir occasionally for 5 minutes to ensure that the fruit is well distributed. Remove the foam from the surface of the pan before stirring.

8. Pour the jam into hot sterilized jars.

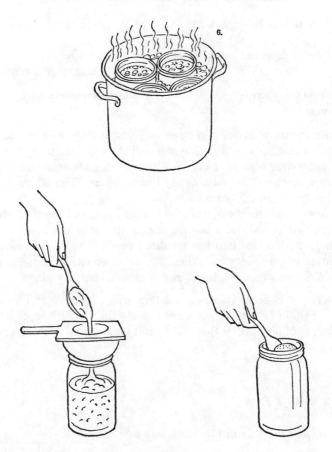

9. Wipe the rims of the jars, making sure there are no drips or seeds sticking to the rim.

10. Cover with a lid or transparent wrap held in place with a rubber band. Label and store in a cool, dry place.

STRAWBERRY JAM

All berry jams are made in exactly the same way.

MAKES 5 8-OUNCE JARS

4 cups sliced strawberries
3 cups sugar

1 tablespoon lemon juice

Place the strawberries in a large, heavy saucepan. Add the sugar and stir over low heat only until the sugar has dissolved. Then bring to a boiling point rapidly over high heat and boil steadily for about 20 minutes until the mixture reaches 220° on a candy thermometer. Skim off the foam occasionally with a slotted spoon.

Remove from the heat, add the lemon juice, and leave to stand for 5 minutes. Stir occasionally to ensure that the strawberries are well distributed. Ladle the jam into hot sterilized jars and seal immediately with a thin layer of paraffin wax. When the wax has set, cover with another thin layer. Cover with a lid. Label and store in a cool, dry place.

COMMENT: It is preferable to use 2 thin layers rather than 1 thick layer of wax. The thin layers will set more quickly than a thick layer and there is less danger of air pockets that will permit the entry of bacteria and cause the jam to spoil.

CHERRY JAM

Plum jam is made in the same way as cherry jam.

MAKES 5 8-OUNCE JARS

4 cups sour cherries
¼ cup water

3 cups sugar
1 tablespoon lemon juice

Remove the cherry pits and crack them with a hammer. Tie the pits and kernels into a piece of cheesecloth. Place the cherries, cherry pits, water and sugar in a heavy pan. Stir over low heat until the cherry juice starts to run and the sugar has dissolved. Bring to boiling point rapidly and continue with the directions for making strawberry jam. Discard the cheesecloth bag when the jam is completed, and add the lemon juice.

COMMENT: Pectin is stored in the skins, cores, and pits of many fruits. The pits are boiled with the fruit to extract the pectin and aid in the "setting" of the jam.

Sweet black cherries are low in pectin, so make the jam in the same way, add 1 tablespoon bottled pectin to the completed jam, and boil for 1 minute.

PEACH AND APRICOT JAMS

Peach and apricot are made in almost exactly the same way as straw-berry jam and cherry jam.

2 pounds peaches or apricots	1 tablespoon lemon juice
3 cups sugar	

Plunge the peaches or apricots in boiling water, a few at a time. Boil for 10 seconds. Drain and plunge the fruit into a bowl of cold water. Remove the skins. Slice the fruit and reserve a few of the pits. Tie the pits in a piece of cheesecloth. (There will be 4 cups of sliced fruit.) Continue with the recipe for strawberry jam. Discard the cheesecloth bag when the jam is completed.

MIXED FRUIT JAMS

A variety of fruits can be combined to make extremely flavorful and utterly marvelous jams.

Measure 4 cups of the prepared fruit and add 3 cups of sugar and 1 tablespoon of lemon juice.

FOR EXAMPLE:

Strawberries, raspberries, blackberries, and apples
Rhubarb and strawberries
Apples and blackberries
Orange and pineapple
Peaches and raspberries

⅍ MAKING JELLY ⅊

Jellies are made from fruit juices boiled with sugar. The juice must be at boiling point when the sugar is added. See following note on adding pectin to jams and jellies. If, in the pectin test, a clump of gel is formed, add ¾ cup of sugar for every cup of juice. If a gel is not formed or is incomplete, add only ½ cup of sugar for each cup of juice. Add 1 teaspoon of lemon juice to every cup of very sweet juice.

❧ NOTE ON ADDING PECTIN ❧
TO JELLIES

Lemon juice is added to make the fruit more acid and ensure that jam and jellies will set. As fruit ripens the acid and pectin are converted to sugar. If you are unsure of the pectin content of fruit, before adding any sugar, stir together 1 tablespoon of the boiled unsweetened juice from the fruit with 1 tablespoon of 70 per cent grain alcohol. If the mixture forms into a single clump, no pectin or lemon juice need be added. If it does not "set" or forms small globules, stir into the completed jam 1 tablespoon commercially bottled pectin or 1 tablespoon lemon juice. (The lemon juice is used when globules form but not a complete clump of gel.) Add 1 tablespoon of pectin to 4 cups of low pectin fruit.

❧ TESTING THE JELLY ❧

Jams and jellies are guaranteed to set if they are boiled until they reach 212° on a candy thermometer. However, it is wise to test the jelly a few degrees lower than that, because a few jellies are ready to set at a lower temperature. Dip a cold, clean metal spoon into the jelly and tip most of the jelly back into the pan. If the last 2 or 3 drops run together and drop from the rim of the spoon as a single sheet, the jelly is ready for setting.

A third test is the "wrinkle" test. Pour a spoonful of jelly onto a saucer and place it in the freezer for 5 minutes. Push your finger through the jelly. If it wrinkles and remains firmly parted, the jelly is ready. Remove the jelly from the heat while making this test or the only perfect jelly you will have is the spoonful in the saucer.

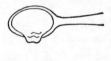

CRAB APPLE JELLY

All jellies made from "hard" fruits rather than berries are made in exactly the same way. MAKES 6 8-OUNCE JARS

4 pounds crab apples **Sugar**

Remove the blossom ends from the crab apples. Cut each apple, unpeeled, into quarters, cutting through the core. Place in a large, heavy pan. Add sufficient cold water to barely cover the apples. Bring to boiling point. Lower the heat and simmer until the crab apples have softened.

Line a strainer with a clean linen kitchen towel, folded, or several layers of cheesecloth. Strain the apple juice through the cloth. It is best to let the juices drip overnight, as this will decrease the temptation to squeeze the apples to try and hurry the process. It cannot be hurried. All that will happen if you squeeze the apples will be that the juice will be cloudy (though if you are in a great hurry you could use an electric juice extractor).

Measure the juice and bring it to boiling point. Add ¾ cup of sugar for every cup of juice. Stir to dissolve and continue boiling gently until it reaches jelling point or 220° on a candy thermometer.

Pour jelly into hot sterilized jars and seal with paraffin wax.

Wine may be substituted for water in extracting juice from firm fruits.

Fruits such as grapes or sliced peaches look exotic suspended in the jelly. Add the fruit after the jelly reaches setting stage and stir into the jelly for 5 minutes to ensure that it is evenly suspended.

GRAPE JELLY

Grape jelly is made in exactly the same way as crab apple jelly (see above). Remove the stems from the grapes. Cut each grape in half to allow the juices to run. Barely cover with cold water. Simmer for approximately 10 minutes and strain the grapes and juice through several thicknesses of cheesecloth. Add ¾ cup of sugar for every cup of juice.

BERRY JELLY

Combine 2 cups of berry juice obtained by puréeing and then straining the fruit with 2 cups of bottled apple juice. Bring to boiling point and add 3 cups of sugar and boil until it reaches 220° on a candy thermometer or until jelling point is reached. Add 3 ounces liquid pectin and boil for 1 minute.

COMMENT: Jelly is most successfully made in small batches, 4 cups or less.

Jellies may be flavored with herbs (mint or rose geranium leaves, or with spices, cloves or cinnamon). Use 1 tablespoon of chopped fresh herbs to 2 cups of juice. Add 3 whole cloves or ½ stick cinnamon to 2 cups of juice. Add herbs and spices to raw fruit.

A few drops of food coloring do wonders to improve the appearance of homemade jellies.

1 pound of juicy fruit such as fully ripened peaches or berries will yield 1 cup of juice and when the sugar has been added will result in 1 cup of jelly.

MARMALADE

Marmalade can be made from oranges, lemons, or grapefruit, either alone or in combination. If you do not have a meat grinder, slice and chop the fruit by hand.

1 orange, preferably a Seville orange	**1 grapefruit**
1 lemon	**Sugar**

Wash the fruit and cut into small pieces. Force the pieces through a meat grinder or chop finely. Reserve the pips. Measure the pulp and fruit juice. Add 3 cups of cold water to every cup of combined pulp and juice. Cover and chill for 24 hours. Transfer to a large, heavy pan and bring to boiling point. Boil for 10 minutes. Cool and chill for another 24 hours. Measure the pulp and juice again. Bring to boiling point and add ¾ cup of sugar to every cup of measured pulp and juice. Boil until a candy thermometer reading of 220° is reached. This is the point at which a jelly will form.

Ladle into hot sterilized jars. Cover with 2 thin layers of melted paraffin wax. Cover with a lid. Label the marmalade and store in a cool, dry place.

CREPES

❧ CREPES ❦

A crepe is a simple thing; it is the batter for Southern fried chicken cooked in a special pan. It is a thin pancake with a high price in a French restaurant. It is a waffle without the egg whites. It is flour and milk, eggs and butter. That is all it is. It is the idea that is so ingenious that several other countries also eat it. The Chinese add water instead of milk and it becomes an egg roll, and the Russians fold it differently and call it a blintz; the Germans and the British call a pancake a pancake; the Italians have another word, but a crepe is merely a vehicle to enclose a filling. Crepes are served for brunch with strawberries and sparkling Burgundy; for lunch with moist morsels of chicken; as an appetizer curled around a creamy lobster and shrimp filling, and for dessert with Susette.

A crepe party is a moderately brilliant notion. A variety of fillings can be kept hot in chafing dishes and similar contraptions, and if you fancy yourself as a showman you can make the crepes in front of the guests so they can be eaten hot from the pan. Within minutes everybody will want to make their own and you can go off and read a book, fall asleep, or be a charming host or hostess.

❧ THE CREPE PAN ❦

It is the crepe pan that makes the crepes. The cook is there merely to add the batter and remove the completed crepes.

The best crepe pans are made of black iron 5 or 6 inches at the base and with shallow flaring sides. Once it has been seasoned, the pan must never be washed or the smooth surface will be ruined, at least temporarily. The crepe pan is a tool for the crepe specialist and should not be used for any other purpose. When the pan is not in use, hide it under the bed or a night prowling visitor may find it and cook up a batch of bacon and eggs. If the integrity of the pan is violated in this manner, try rubbing it gently with a combination of oil and salt. If the surface is not restored you will have to season the pan again.

❧ SEASONING A CREPE OR ❦ OMELETTE PAN

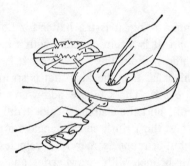

It is usually necessary to season a pan only once, and it will last for your lifetime and for those of your heirs, who will fight to inherit it.

Wash the pan in soapy water and scrub it with a nylon pad. Rinse it in clear water, dry it, and fill it ¾ full with vegetable oil. Place over low heat for 20 minutes. Remove the pan from the heat and leave to stand for 24 hours. Tip out the oil. Wipe with paper towels. Cover with transparent wrap and paste a label on the wrap saying something to the effect that the wrath of the heavens will rain boulders upon the head of him who touches the pan, the fires of destruction will scourge and castigate him, and evil and pestilence will surround the rest of his days. If you have a small label you could write fewer words.

Between uses the pan is wiped with paper towels.

❧ FILLING FOR CREPES ❦

Almost any foods can be surrounded by a sauce and filled into a crepe. However, the mixture must be thick enough to hold its shape or it will be difficult to handle.

Garnish the completed crepes with a little of the reserved filling, spread across the crepe at the last moment. For instance, garnish spinach crepes with a broad swath of creamed spinach; garnish seafood crepes with a shrimp with its head and coat on; and decorate dessert crepes with fruit or powdered sugar.

CREPE BATTER

MAKES 14 CREPES

¾ cup all-purpose flour   1 egg
¼ teaspoon salt   1 egg yolk
1 cup milk   2 tablespoons melted butter

Place all the ingredients in the blender and blend for 10 seconds until smooth. The batter may be used immediately or kept in the refrigerator. It will thicken as it stands, so you may need to add another tablespoon or two of milk.

✍ HOW TO MAKE CREPES ✍

Pour about a tablespoon of oil into the pan. Place the pan over moderate heat and swirl the oil in the pan to coat the bottom and sides. Tip out the oil.

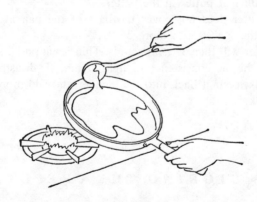

Select a shallow-bowled kitchen spoon and ladle a spoonful of batter sufficient to make a paper-thin layer. Tip out any excess batter, the crepe itself will remain holding to the bottom of the pan. Cook the crepe until it has a dull appearance and loses its shine. This will take about one and one half minutes. Small bubbles will appear around the edges of the crepe, and the underside will be lightly browned. Slide a metal spatula under the crepe and flip it onto the other side. Cook the crepe for about one minute on the second side.

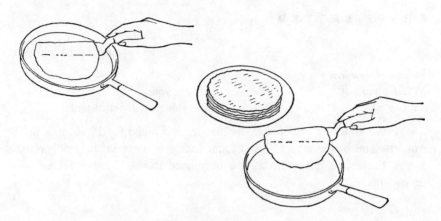

Cover a wire cooling rack with a folded kitchen towel. Stack the crepes on the towel with the second sides facing up so they will be ready for filling. The second side is never as beautiful as the first side, but this should not concern you because it will not be visible when the crepe is filled.

If the batter forms a clump in the center, the pan is too hot. Wave it about like a flag until it cools slightly. Add a teaspoon of oil and carry on. It is not necessary to add oil to the pan before making each crepe, as there is sufficient butter in the batter.

If the batter does not cover the base of the pan evenly but forms holes, fill in the spaces with more batter.

The batter will thicken as it stands. Thin it with additional milk. The batter should be the consistency of light cream. If, disastrously, you add too much milk, pour it back into the blender and add more flour and another egg yolk.

⧖ STORING THE CREPES ⧗

Crepes can be kept in a plastic bag in the refrigerator either filled or unfilled. They can also be frozen. Frozen crepes keep best when they are filled. Unfilled, they tend to become dry and have a decided tendency to break when they are rolled around a filling.

LEFTOVER CREPE BATTER

Leftover crepe batter can be used for making batter-fried chicken, French-fried onions, and fruit fritters.

❧ HOW TO SHAPE CREPES ❦

 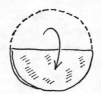

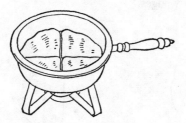

SEAFOOD CREPES

FOR 4 FOR LUNCH
FOR 6 AS AN APPETIZER

Preheat oven to 350°.

1 cup cooked lobster cut into small
 pieces

¼ pound bay scallops
¼ pound small shrimp

SAUCE

2 tablespoons butter
2 tablespoons flour
1½ cups milk
2 teaspoons tomato paste

2 tablespoons freshly grated
 Parmesan cheese
1 tablespoon white vermouth

GARNISH

Parsley

Lemon wedges

Place the lobster in a bowl. Simmer the scallops and shrimp in salted water for 5 minutes. Drain. Add the scallops to the lobster. Shell the shrimp, devein them, and add to the lobster. Reserve 6 shrimp in their shells.

To prepare the sauce, heat the butter. Add the flour and cook for 1 minute. Stir in the milk with a wire whisk to form a medium-thick sauce. Stir in the tomato paste, cheese, and vermouth.

Add ⅓ of the sauce to the combined seafood. Fill the crepes: place a spoonful of the mixture slightly off center and roll up like a cigar.

Place the filled crepes in a buttered 9 x 13″ baking dish and dot the surface with butter. Bake in a preheated oven for 20 minutes until very hot.

Heat the remaining sauce and spoon over the crepes in a long line. Garnish the crepes with reserved shrimp and garnish the dish with parsley clusters and lemon wedges.

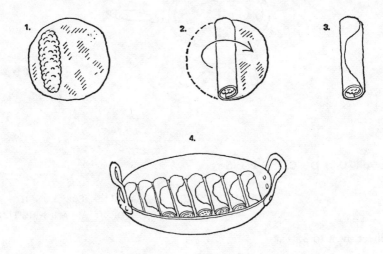

CHICKEN CREPES

An appetizer.   FOR 6

Preheat oven to 350°.

Recipe for crepe batter (see Index)
  2 **cups roasted chicken cut into small pieces**

½ **cup bean sprouts or ½ cup peas, cooked**
2-ounce jar pimientos, chopped

SAUCE

  2 **tablespoons butter**
  2 **tablespoons flour**
1½ **cups milk**
  3 **tablespoons finely chopped parsley**

2 **teaspoons lemon juice**
½ **teaspoon salt**
Freshly ground black pepper

Prepare the crepes. Place the chicken, bean sprouts or peas, and pimientos in a bowl.

To prepare the sauce, heat the butter. Add the flour and stir in the milk with a wire whisk to form a smooth sauce. Add the parsley and lemon juice. Season with salt and pepper.

Add ⅓ of the sauce to the chicken mixture. Place a spoonful of the filling in each crepe. Roll the crepe into a cigar shape and place in a 9 x 13″ buttered baking pan. Dot the surface with butter and place in a preheated oven for 20 minutes.

Heat the remaining sauce and spoon over the crepes.

HAM AND ASPARAGUS CREPES

An appetizer. FOR 6

Preheat oven to 350°.

Recipe for crepe batter (see Index)	**1 pound thin asparagus spears,**
¼ pound thinly sliced boiled ham	**cooked**
	Hollandaise Sauce (see Index)

Prepare the crepes. Line each crepe with ham and trim the edges so it fits neatly. Lay 2 asparagus spears over the ham and add a teaspoon of hollandaise sauce. Roll the crepes and place in a buttered baking dish. Dot the surface with butter and bake in a preheated oven for 10 minutes. Top with hollandaise sauce.

⤝ SUGGESTIONS FOR OTHER ⤞ CREPE FILLINGS

2 cups of Ratatouille   see Index

Chicken Livers in Madeira Sauce   see Index

Kidneys in Mustard Sauce   see Index

Cherries Jubilee   see Index

Strawberries Romanoff   see Index

BLUEBERRY CREPES

FOR 6

Preheat oven to 350°.

Recipe for crepe batter (see Index)
2 boxes blueberries
2 tablespoons red currant jelly
½ cup orange juice
½ teaspoon cinnamon

1 tablespoon cornstarch dissolved
    in 2 tablespoons cold water
Butter
Powdered sugar
Whipped cream

Prepare the crepes.

Place the blueberries in a saucepan. Add the red currant jelly, orange juice, and cinnamon. Simmer for 10 minutes. Stir in the cornstarch dissolved in cold water.

Fill each crepe with 2 tablespoons of the blueberry mixture, roll into cigar shapes, and place in a buttered 9 x 13″ baking pan. There will be some of the mixture left over. Dot the surface with butter and arrange remaining blueberries around the sides of the dish.

Bake in a preheated oven for 15 minutes. Dust with sifted powdered sugar and serve with mounds of whipped cream.

CREPES SUZETTE

A specialty of the house.

FOR 4

Crepe batter (see Index)
6 tablespoons superfine sugar
8 tablespoons butter, softened
Grated rind and juice of 1 orange

Grated rind of 1 lemon
2 tablespoons Grand Marnier
2 tablespoons brandy

Prepare the crepes.

Combine 4 tablespoons of the sugar with the butter, grated rind and strained orange juice, grated lemon rind, and Grand Marnier.

When ready to serve the crepes, place the orange butter in a chafing dish or frying pan over moderate heat. Roll each crepe in the hot butter and fold in half and then in half again. Leave to one side of the pan. Continue until all the crepes have been added and folded.

Spread the crepes over bottom of the pan, and sprinkle with the remaining 2 tablespoons sugar. Heat the brandy in a small pot. Light with a match and pour the flames over the crepes. Serve immediately.

OMELETTES

≥ OMELETTES ≤

The most perfect omelette is made in less than three minutes, so, if you have a few eggs you can feed yourself, your friends, and neighbors quickly and triumphantly at any time of the day or night. However, in addition to the eggs, you will need an omelette pan. Even with the best of intentions, the freshest of eggs and the most dazzling of fillings, you cannot make an omelette without an omelette pan. In fact, this is a slight exaggeration that perhaps should be modified to say that some people can do it but I cannot. But then some people can play a violin concerto or add a row of figures accurately while others must resort to record players and adding machines. In short, an omelette pan makes the entire procedure infinitely easier, and, if you are fond of omelettes, it is recommended that you own an omelette pan.

≥ THE OMELETTE PAN ≤

The pan may be made of iron or aluminum. It should have rounded sides that curve slightly inward at the top. This will prevent the eggs from spilling as they are stirred rapidly in the pan.

The best omelettes are made for one person so that the eggs will cook and set quickly and enable the omelette to be unmolded onto the plate easily. A pan with a base diameter of five and one half or six inches is the perfect size for a two-egg omelette.

An omelette pan, like a small boy, should be loved and cherished and never washed. A well-seasoned omelette pan will permit the eggs to slide around without sticking. For the directions on how to season an omelette pan see the Index.

HOW TO MAKE AN OMELETTE FOR ONE

2 eggs	**Freshly ground black pepper**
¼ teaspoon salt	**1 tablespoon butter**

Break the eggs into a bowl. Season with salt and pepper and beat lightly with a fork.

Heat the butter in the omelette pan. As it heats, large bubbles will appear and then subside to be replaced with tiny bubbles about the size of a heady champagne bubble. At this point the butter is almost ready to burn.

Add the eggs immediately and stir them rapidly with a fork. Hold the tines of the fork parallel with the bottom of the pan as though making scrambled eggs. As the eggs begin to form curds, stop stirring and spread the eggs over the bottom of the pan to form a smooth layer.

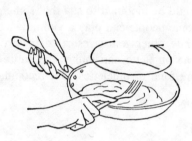

Place a spoonful of the filling across the pan on the side opposite from the handle. Tilt the pan away from you and slide a spatula under the un-filled portion of the omelette. Fold this half over the filled half.

Slide the omelette back to the center of the pan and allow the under-side to brown slightly for a minute.

Now, to get the omelette safely out of the pan. Reverse your grip on the handle of the pan so your thumb is on top. Hold the pan at a 45° angle to the plate. Invert the pan over the plate and the omelette, rounded golden and beautiful, will now be resting happily on the plate.

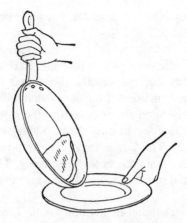

Brush the top of the omelette with melted butter to make it even shinier, and garnish with parsley sprigs, cherry tomatoes, black olives, or any other colorful good-tasting things you can conjure up.

COMMENT: Almost all cookbooks imply that nothing ever goes wrong in the kitchen. Though this is a moderately reasonable assumption when directions are followed carefully, it is a fact that it is the rare person who does things properly all the time. If your first omelette refuses to leave the pan, if your first batch of jam is a miserable disaster, and if your soufflé, instead of reaching for the stars, cowers at the bottom of the dish, do not despair. Well, despair at the time, but do not let it daunt you from trying again. It happens. Not only does it happen but if you are really honest you will possibly be able to admit that you know why it happened: a) you burned the butter or decided not to season the omelette pan, b) you added too much sugar to the jam, c) you opened the door of the oven six times to see how the soufflé was getting along without you. Try again. After you have mastered the techniques, they will last a lifetime, and even though the truth of the old cliché about the way to a man's heart can be disputed, even rejected, it is nice to know you can make an omelette whenever you want to.

⚮ MAKING OMELETTES FOR GUESTS ⚮

As the best omelettes are cooked one at a time, making several at once poses something of a problem to which there are several solutions other than changing the menu.

1. You could buy a larger omelette pan and compromise your principles and your omelettes.

2. A better plan is to buy two or even three omelette pans. Break two eggs into a bowl, stir them with a fork and find a ladle or measuring cup that accommodates the eggs exactly, then break the required number of eggs for the required number of omelettes that will be needed into the bowl. The ladle will be used for transferring the eggs into the pans and saves time cracking the eggs, beating them, adding salt and pepper, and disposing of the shells. The butter may also be divided into tablespoon parts and placed where you can reach them easily. The filling, or various fillings, can be prepared in advance and kept warm over another burner or in chafing dishes.

3. Now you can institute an assembly line. The butter is melting in one pan while the eggs are being stirred in another. The filling is added while the other omelette is browning. This system works extremely well as long as nobody speaks to you and if somebody else is delegated to answer the telephone or the door.

4. Another plan is to cook the omelettes in front of the guests on a portable burner. The omelette fillings will be made in advance. Even though this takes exactly the same length of time as working in the kitchen, there are certain clear advantages to this approach: a) you are obviously working hard at preparing the omelettes, which encourages everybody else to be gratefully patient, b) it provides a degree of entertainment value, hopefully of the purest variety, c) it inspires people to make their own, having watched you, the expert. At this point you may adopt the air of a consultant.

❧ FILLINGS FOR OMELETTES ❦

Almost anything that is good to eat can be tucked into an omelette: a handful of grated cheese, a little leftover chicken, some cooked vegetables, or a tablespoon of fresh herbs. The quantities in the following recipes are for two, two-egg omelettes. When the recipe suggests using one cooked potato and four strips of crumbled bacon and you have neither a potato nor bacon but only a fresh tomato and some dried herbs, use them instead. It is the principle of the thing that counts and there must be something in the refrigerator you could use for a filling. There are, however, two things to remember: any ingredients in a sauce, such as a spoonful of leftover stew, must be thick enough to hold their shape, otherwise the sauce will run under the folded omelette and fry on the bottom of the omelette pan. This will make the omelette stick and ruin the surface of the pan. If this should happen, unmold the omelette as best you can and rub the offending spot with salt. If this does not restore the surface, the pan must be reseasoned.

The other thing to remember is that hot fillings must be hot because the cooking time inside the omelette is very brief.

OMELETTE WITH HERBS

For each omelette add 2 tablespoons combined fresh herbs, e.g., 1 tablespoon chopped parsley, 2 teaspoons chopped chives, ½ teaspoon tarragon. Use half the quantity of dried herbs. Add the herbs to the eggs, salt, and pepper and follow the directions on how to make an omelette. Other herbs such as dill, basil, marjoram, and oregano may also be used.

CHEESE OMELETTE

For each omelette use ¼ cup grated Cheddar, or combine Swiss and Parmesan or other hard grated cheeses. If using soft cheeses cut into tiny cubes. Follow the directions on how to make an omelette and add the cheese at the point that a smooth layer of eggs is formed.

OMELETTE BONNE FEMME

For each omelette use:

4 slices bacon	**1 small raw potato sliced or**
1 tablespoon butter	**2 tablespoons mashed potatoes**
¼ cup chopped onion	

Fry the bacon until crisp. Drain and crumble the bacon. Heat the butter and fry the onion and sliced potato until cooked, or add mashed potatoes and heat until hot.

Follow the directions on how to make an omelette and add all the filling ingredients at the point that a smooth layer of eggs is formed.

MUSHROOM OMELETTE

For each omelette use:

¼ cup sliced mushrooms   1 tablespoon butter
1 tablespoon finely chopped onion

Fry the mushrooms and onion in hot butter until soft and tender. Follow the directions on how to make an omelette and add the mushrooms and onion at the point that a smooth layer of eggs is formed.

HAM AND SPINACH OMELETTE

1 teaspoon butter   Sprinkle of freshly grated nutmeg
¼ cup cooked chopped spinach   1 teaspoon lemon juice
1 slice boiled ham, chopped into
  small pieces

Place all the ingredients in a small saucepan and heat until hot. Follow the directions on how to make an omelette and add the filling ingredients at the point that a smooth layer of eggs is formed.

OTHER OMELETTE FILLINGS

See suggestions for crepe fillings as listed in the Index.

* ¼ cup tuna fish, 1 teaspoon lemon juice, 1 tablespoon mayonnaise.

* ¼ cup salmon, 1 tablespoon hollandaise sauce if it is already made, or 1 teaspoon of lemon juice and 1 tablespoon mayonnaise.

* 1 tablespoon canned pesto. Top omelette with sour cream.

* ¼ cup finely cut smoked salmon, 2 tablespoons thinly sliced cream cheese.

* Top omelette with caviar and sour cream.

* Cooked zucchini and roasted peppers. Top with grated Parmesan cheese.

SOUFFLÉS

❧ SOUFFLÉS ❧

There is an aura of luxury surrounding certain foods. I am not speaking so much of things like caviar and champagne, but simple foods like eggs. There is no comparison, for instance, between a poached egg on toast, good as it is, and eggs Benedict or *oeufs en gelée*. Yet all these dishes are founded on a straightforward poached egg. The same is true for a soufflé. Anybody can make a cheese sauce, but add some beaten egg whites to it and there you have something. Though really few things are less trouble to make than a simple sauce, nevertheless the idea of making a soufflé strikes fear and terror into the bravest of hearts. Yet see how easy it is. . . .

❧ SOUFFLÉ DISHES ❧

A soufflé can be made in any dish. However, it is best in a soufflé dish, best because part of the beauty of a soufflé lies in its appearance. A good soufflé should rise 2″ above the rim of the dish. A spectacular soufflé will rise 6″ above the rim. In order to perform this sleight of hand, achieved merely by adding more egg whites, the soufflé will have a little support in the form of a collar tied around the dish. So though you can make a splendid soufflé in a teacup with a broken handle, it will certainly lose some of its visual impact and be merely a ho-hum pudding.

Soufflé dishes are made in various sizes, ranging from miniature ones for 3-day-old babies to 2-quart dishes for serving 6 hearty adults. If you are only contemplating one dish select a 1½-quart dish. It will be perfect for 4 people. If you are making a soufflé for two, cut the recipe in half, use individual soufflé dishes, and reduce the cooking time to 25 minutes.

❧ HOW TO PREPARE THE ❧ SOUFFLÉ DISH

Butter the dish generously. For an entree soufflé sprinkle the buttered dish with flour or grated cheese. For a dessert soufflé sprinkle with flour and sugar.

Tear off a piece of wax paper large enough to encircle the dish and leave a 2″ overlap. Fold the paper in half lengthwise and make another ¼″ crease at the folded edge for increased rigidity. Butter and flour the top third of the paper. Butter the 2″ overlap so that the paper will stick to itself. Tie the paper around the dish with string.

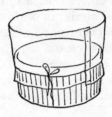

❧ HOW TO MAKE A SOUFFLÉ ☙

Preheat oven to 375°.

Melt the butter in a heavy pan. Stir in the flour and cook for 1 minute. Add the milk, or other liquid, gradually, stirring with a wire whisk to form a smooth sauce. (This is now a thick basic white sauce.)

Remove from the heat and add the egg yolks one at a time. (This is now an enriched white sauce.)

Add the cheese (this is now an enriched cheese or Mornay sauce) or add other meats or alternative ingredients. Add the seasonings.

Place the egg whites in a bowl. Add the cream of tartar and salt to stabilize the egg whites. Beat the egg whites until they stand in soft peaks. Fold the egg whites into the sauce. (This is now a soufflé.) Do not attempt to stir the egg whites into the sauce too vigorously or all the air, which makes the soufflé rise, will escape. Leave oases of egg whites; they will disappear in the cooking.

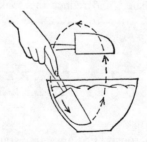

Place in the center of a preheated oven and bake for 35 minutes. Bake individual soufflés for 25 minutes.

COMMENT: The soufflé can be prepared in advance. Leave the ingredients at room temperature. Do not chill the basic mixture or it will become too firm and consequently it is difficult to add the egg white. Ideally a soufflé should be made from start to finish without interruption.

Also, if you decide to make a soufflé for 12 people, do not double the recipe but instead make 2 separate soufflés, for they will rise better and the cooking time is easier to estimate.

⚘ TESTING THE SOUFFLÉ ⚘

There is a sure and infallible way of testing a soufflé, a quiche, a cake, and similar preparations without opening the oven door, assuming you have a light in the oven, a glass window in the oven door, and a slightly uneven kitchen floor. Almost everybody has a slightly uneven kitchen floor. Turn on the oven light and knock your fist against the window. If the soufflé is ready nothing will happen. Take it out and eat it. If it is not yet ready it will quiver and wobble uneasily in the center. Turn off the light and go away for 5 minutes.

If you do not have a window in the oven door, shake the soufflé, with utmost caution and gentleness, and the same effect will occur. Close the oven door and increase the heat by five degrees to compensate for the heat loss in opening the door.

Toothpicks, though satisfactory for poking at quiches or cakes, are useless for testing a soufflé. Use a knitting needle, a chopstick or similar prodding device if you are unhappy with the quivering test. If after almost total immersion in the soufflé it comes out clean, the soufflé is ready. Some people like soufflés runny in the middle but they collapse very quickly in that state.

⚘ HOW TO SERVE A SOUFFLÉ ⚘

Seat the guests and let them toy with a forkful of dainty morsels. The guests must await the soufflé, not the other way around.

Take the soufflé from the oven as soon as it is ready. If you try and postpone the moment of readiness by lowering the heat of the oven, the soufflé will know it is not being treated with respect and will promptly collapse.

Remove the paper collar and tie a starched white linen napkin around the bowl if you wish to be very fancy. Carry the soufflé to the table. Everybody will gasp with wonder. Do not heed them but promptly take the two spoons you have thoughtfully remembered to put on the table. Place the spoons back to back and enter the top center of the soufflé. Pull the spoons towards the sides to allow the steam to escape and serve it immediately. Each moment of delay will diminish the soufflé, for it is merely a castle in the air and you cannot linger to admire the architecture.

PLAN FOR SOUFFLÉS FOR FOUR PEOPLE

Use a 1½-quart (6 cup) soufflé dish.

2 tablespoons butter
3 tablespoons flour
1 cup milk, chicken broth, beef broth, wine, beer, or fruit juice
4 egg yolks
¾ cup grated cheese, shredded cooked meat, chicken, fish, or cooked sliced vegetables

1–2 tablespoons herbs, mustard, tomato paste, or other seasonings
6 egg whites
⅛ teaspoon cream of tartar
¼ teaspoon salt

For dessert soufflés use:

¾ cup chopped or sliced fruit
¼ cup sugar

2 tablespoons fruit liqueur

CHICKEN SOUFFLÉ

FOR 4

Preheat oven to 375°.

2 tablespoons butter	½ teaspoon tarragon
3 tablespoons flour	6 egg whites
1¼ cups milk	¼ teaspoon salt
4 egg yolks	⅛ teaspoon cream of tartar
¾ cup diced cooked chicken	

To prepare the soufflé dish, butter a 1½-quart straight-sided dish and sprinkle with flour. Tear off a piece of wax paper large enough to encircle the dish and allow a 2″ overlap. Fold the paper in half lengthwise and make a ½″ fold at the folded edge for additional rigidity. Butter the top third of the paper including the overlap and sprinkle with flour. Tie the paper around the outside of the dish with a piece of string.

Heat the butter in a saucepan. Stir in the flour and add the milk gradually to obtain a smooth sauce. Remove the pan from the heat and stir in the egg yolks. Add the chicken and tarragon.

Place the egg whites in a bowl and add salt and cream of tartar. Beat until the egg whites stand in stiff peaks. Fold the egg whites into the chicken mixture gently. (Do not stir too much or the air that has been beaten into the egg whites will escape.)

Transfer the mixture to the prepared soufflé dish and place in a preheated oven. Close the door and creep quietly away. Come back in 30 minutes and the soufflé will have risen to the top of the oven. Serve the soufflé immediately.

COMMENT: As you will see if you look at the recipe critically, a soufflé is merely a pretentious sauce that takes such a huge gulp of egg whites it becomes puffed up with its own importance.

PLAN FOR SOUFFLÉS FOR SIX PEOPLE

Use a 2-quart (8 cup) soufflé dish.

3 tablespoons butter
4 tablespoons flour
1½ cups milk, chicken broth, beef broth, wine, beer, or fruit juice
6 egg yolks
1¼ cups grated cheese, shredded cooked meat, chicken, fish, or cooked sliced vegetables

1½ teaspoons herbs, mustard, tomato paste, or other seasonings
8 egg whites
⅛ teaspoon cream of tartar
¼ teaspoon salt

For dessert soufflés use:

1¼ cups chopped or sliced fruit
⅓ cup sugar

3 tablespoons fruit liqueur

CHEESE SOUFFLÉ

FOR 6

Preheat oven to 375°.

2 tablespoons butter
3 tablespoons flour
1 cup milk
4 egg yolks
¾ cup grated Cheddar cheese or
 ½ cup grated Swiss cheese and
 ¼ cup Parmesan cheese

1 teaspoon mustard
¼ teaspoon nutmeg
6 egg whites
⅛ teaspoon cream of tartar
¼ teaspoon salt

Follow the preceding directions for how to make a soufflé.

CURRIED SHRIMP SOUFFLÉ

FOR 6

2 tablespoons butter
2 teaspoons curry powder
3 tablespoons flour
1 cup milk
4 egg yolks

¾ cup cooked shrimp cut into small pieces
1 teaspoon tomato paste
6 egg whites
⅛ teaspoon cream of tartar
¼ teaspoon salt

Heat the butter in a heavy pan. Stir in the curry powder and cook for 1 minute to release the flavor. Stir in the flour. Continue with the preceding directions for how to make a soufflé.

OTHER SUGGESTIONS FOR FLAVORING SOUFFLÉS

Keep all the ingredients for making a soufflé in a 1½-quart dish in the same proportions and add the following ingredients at the point where the seasonings are added.

SPINACH SOUFFLÉ

* Fry chopped onion in the butter, stir in the flour, proceed with the preceding directions for how to make a soufflé, and add ¾ cup chopped cooked spinach and 2 teaspoons lemon juice.

HERB SOUFFLÉ

* ½ cup finely chopped fresh parsley, ¼ cup finely chopped chives, 1 teaspoon fresh tarragon (use ½ quantity of dried tarragon).

HAM SOUFFLÉ

* ¾ cup finely chopped ham, 2 teaspoons mustard.

DESSERT SOUFFLÉS

* See plan for making soufflés.

TANGERINE AND SLICED ALMOND SOUFFLÉ

¾ cup drained canned tangerines, 2 ounces sliced almonds, 1 teaspoon almond extract, ¼ cup sugar.

GRAND MARNIER SOUFFLÉ

Make basic soufflé, omitting ¾ cup filling. Flavor soufflé with 2 teaspoons vanilla, ¼ cup sugar, and 3 tablespoons Grand Marnier.

CHERRY SOUFFLÉ

¾ cup pitted canned or fresh cherries, cut in half, ¼ cup sugar, and 2 tablespoons kirsch.

APRICOT SOUFFLÉ

¾ cup puréed canned apricots, 1 teaspoon almond extract, 2 tablespoons apricot brandy and 2 tablespoons rum.

STRAWBERRY SOUFFLÉ

¾ cup sliced strawberries, ¼ cup sugar, 1 teaspoon vanilla, 2 tablespoons brandy, 5 drops red food coloring.

COMMENT: Dust the surface of all cooked dessert soufflés with sifted powdered sugar and serve with whipped cream.

CHEESE AND WINE

✑ PLANNING A CHEESE AND ✎ WINE PARTY

There are many ways to have a cheese and wine party. It can be designed to further your knowledge of wines from many countries or be restricted to a study of the vineyards.

The party may be arranged so that you can dazzle your guests and confound your neighbors with your knowledge and erudition, or if you know nothing of the subject, you can read and memorize key phrases from a book absorbed the previous evening. Another alternative is to invite an authority on wine to talk to the group. Knowing a little about what you are tasting, how the grape matures, and how it bestows its own distinctive character to the wine increases the pleasure of drinking beyond all measure.

Drinking wine is a serious and at the same time joyous way to spend your life, but you may decide not to be learned and simply settle for a jug of wine, a hunk of cheese, and choose to sit on the floor and enjoy yourselves.

If you are having this type of party, nothing more need be said, for the conversation that will flow from the wine is pleasure enough. So let us concentrate on the serious, or moderately serious, cheese and wine party.

I will not give a specific list of wines and cheeses because it is not realistic to suppose that you can always find a bottle from a particular vineyard and a specific year, and even if you could, wine is a variable thing. Unless you know its history from the time it was bottled to the time it was sold, the wine may be adversely affected by improper storage and exposure to heat or cold, thus affecting the taste and ultimately your opinion of the wine. Also, to give precise suggestions is to imply that there are absolutes in selecting wine and any deviation from the list leaves the impression that there is a right and a wrong wine. In fact the opposite is true. Any wine that you enjoy is the right wine for you, but do not let that hinder your exploration, for that would be like discovering one record and refusing to hear any other music.

It is not surprising to discover that wines and cheeses that grow up together in the same geographical area also taste good together. French wines, complicated and sophisticated, are sublime with French cheeses; cool white Swiss mountain wines are at their peak with hard firm Swiss cheeses; and fruity wines from Italy, Spain, and Portugal are the natural partners for the cheeses of the same country.

Though any wine is enhanced by almost any cheese, a strong cheese can overwhelm a light and delicate wine and vice versa. If there is a rule to be established, serve the soft creamy cheeses first with chilled fragrant white wine and follow a natural course to a grand climax, reserving the greatest, most full-bodied wines of depth and character for the robust and mellow cheeses.

❧ HOW MUCH WINE AND ❧ CHEESE TO BUY

One bottle of wine will serve eight people at a wine-tasting party. So if you have eight wines to taste, each guest will drink about half a bottle. After half a bottle many people stop tasting seriously and begin drinking seriously.

Estimate roughly three ounces of cheese for each guest, though the quantity is dependent on the time of day. At an evening party, after dinner, people will eat less cheese than if it is early evening, and in addition to being politely interested they are also ravenously hungry.

❧ BUYING THE WINE ❧

Try and buy the wine at least a week in advance. Wine, like small boys, is not at its best after even a short journey. The wine gets shaken up and needs time to compose itself again. Try to find a store with a knowledgeable and honest (two entirely separate but essential characteristics) proprietor and seek advice you can trust.

⚛ BUYING THE CHEESE ⚛

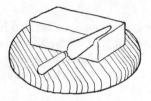

Cheese is much easier to buy than wine because you can taste it in the shop. Do not under any circumstances be intimidated by the storekeeper wielding a knife. If you do not like the cheese, do not buy it no matter how hard he is trying to get rid of it. Bad cheese is his responsibility; do not let it become yours. Buy the cheeses on the day you plan to serve them because the storage facilities are usually better in a cheese shop than in a home refrigerator, where they tend to pick up other flavors.

⚛ CHOOSING THE GLASSES ⚛

Wineglasses should be made of clear glass, so you can see the wine and not be forced to admire the color of the glass. The glasses must be large or enormous. Small glasses should be scorned in direct proportion to their meager capacity. They are for those who equate wine with sin and have no place in anybody's home. Fill a small glass to the utmost brim, raise it with trembling fingers, fearful of spilling a drop, to your lips and the wine is gone. Ask for more when the glass is empty and you are filled with guilt. After four glasses totaling barely a sip of wine, you have to refuse a tentatively phrased offer of yet more (a negative response based more on moral compunction than gastronomic fulfillment).

Large wineglasses should be only half filled, so you may fill your senses with all the blossoming fragrance that is part of the pleasure of drinking wine.

Invest in a couple of beautiful glasses even if you plan to drink only cheap and cheerful wine for the length of your days. An exquisite glass enhances even the most modest of wines. For a cheese and wine party rent or borrow good glasses if necessary.

❧ SERVING THE CHEESE AND WINE ❧

Chill the white wine and champagne for two hours in the refrigerator. Do not serve them too cold or part of the flavor of the wine is lost. More people have headaches from drinking wine that is too cold than from drinking too much wine. Serve the white wines first with the mildest cheeses.

Open the red wines an hour before they are to be served to allow them to soften as they come in contact with the air. Serve the best wines last.

Serve even the creamiest cheeses at room temperature.

Serve the wine and cheese with crusty bread or a variety of homemade breads. Crackers are all right if you like them. Some people like butter with bread and cheese, and though this habit should not be encouraged, a small bowl of unsalted butter could be put on the table in a not too obvious spot. Olives, radishes, celery, carrot sticks, and other tastes should not be served at a serious wine-tasting party, as they distort the flavor of both the cheese and wine but are fine for decorative purposes and somebody might eat them.

❧ TASTING THE WINE ❧

The only way to learn about wine is to drink it regularly and thoughtfully. Gradually, as your knowledge increases, your palate will change and become more refined.

In a culture that is weaned on Coca-Cola it is easy to stumble upon a Cold Duck or Annie Greenspring, a pink and wildly alcoholic bubbly lady. In the early days of discovering wine even Old Boones liquor farm does not seem a bad place to be. But none of these can compare with the riches of those wines that are natural wines made from grapes that have matured late into the summer and ripened into gloriousness. The so called "pop" wines cannot compare with the light, dry, and fresh-tasting white wines, or a young new Beaujolais drunk within a few weeks of the harvest.

To judge a wine, first look at it in the glass. Notice the color. It may vary between a light clear red to a deep dark burgundy or from a golden amber to a light straw color. Swirl it gently around the glass, sniff it carefully, and notice if it has the fresh fragrance of flowers. Is it musky or spicy?

Taste the wine and it may be light as a goblet of spring water, refreshing enough to be taken in large gulps, or it may fill your mouth with heavy, rounded fullness. Such a wine is for slow sipping, noticing how it softens and mellows as it comes in contact with the air, with your palate, and changes in relation to the food you are eating.

THEMES FOR A CHEESE AND WINE PARTY

A Burgundy Party

Either a) – Look at a wine map and choose all the wines from the Burgundy region of France. Begin a wine tour from the light wines of the Mediterranean and travel on to the noble wines of the Côte d'Or, or

b) – Try the so called "Burgundy wines" of California and New York States and compare them with Spanish, Australian, Chilean, South African, and French Burgundies. Choose one cheese from each group in the list that follows these suggested themes.

A Bordeaux Party

Compare the wines from Médoc, St. Émilion, Pomerol, and Graves. Choose one cheese from each group of cheeses in the list that follows these suggested themes.

California Wine Party

Compare the wines, beginning with the white and ending with red wines, of Gallo, Christian Brothers, Wente, Louis Martini, Mondavi, and other vineyards. Select bottles that have the same varietal names. For example, compare all the Pinot Noirs from different vineyards.

The name of the grape in a vintaged bottle means that at least 75 per cent of those grapes were Pinot Noir. This is not true for a nonvintage bottle, when only 51 per cent of any one type of grape need be used. (You cannot really compare intelligently wines that have meaningless names like California Chablis with a California Gewürtztraminer, because the only true Chablis is made from grapes grown in the region of France.) Serve the wines with North American or Canadian cheeses.

A Sparkling Wine Party

Compare American, Italian, and French sparkling wines at any time of the day. Serve the wines or champagnes with one soft creamy French cheese, one semisoft, and one slicing cheese from Switzerland.

A Sherry Tasting

Compare sherries: dry cocktail and cream sherries in the early evening or before lunch. Serve the sherry with Edam or Gouda cheese.

A Port and Stilton Party

This is good to have in the late evening in December or January, when the Stilton cheese is at its best.

⤳ THE CHEESES ⤦
A small sampler

Soft Cheeses

Cream Cheese — *America*

Neufchâtel — *America*

Crema Danica — *Denmark*

Boursin, Boursault (triple creams) — *France*

Pasteurized Cheese, e.g., Kirsch, Walnut, and Garlic — *France*

Goat Cheeses — *France*

Camembert — *France*

Brie — *France*

Coulommiers — *France*

Pont L'Évêque — *France*

Semisoft Cheeses
St. Paulin — *France*
Port Salut — *France*
Beaumont — *France*
Tomme de Savoie — *France*
Munster — *France*
Munster — *America*
Alpenjoy — *Germany*
Bel Paese — *Italy*
Fontina — *Italy*
Gouda — *Holland*
Edam — *Holland*
Oka — *Canada*

Firm Cheeses
Tilsit — *Germany*
Emmenthal — *Switzerland*
Gruyère — *Switzerland*
Appenzell — *Switzerland*
Cheddar — *England, New York, Canada*
Jarlsberg — *Norway*

Blue Cheeses
Stilton — *England*
Roquefort — *France*
Gorgonzola — *Italy*

There are approximately two thousand other cheeses from which to choose.

AN
ICE-CREAM-PARLOR
PARTY

⚹ AN ICE-CREAM-PARLOR PARTY ⚹

A novel way of surprising guests.

Make several different flavors of ice cream and sauces and let people help themselves. The ice cream can be put in attractive bowls or, for something really spectacular, make an ice-cream bowl and arrange different flavored scoops of ice cream in the bowl. This plan is only practical, however, if you have a large freezer.

To make the ice-cream bowl or mold, select two containers that will nest inside each other. You can use any material, but metal is the most practical for unmolding. If you are using clay, for instance two clay plant pots, line the larger container with plastic. Pour an inch of water into the larger container and freeze until it is solid. Rest the inner container on the ice and fill the space between the two containers with ice water. The ice mold will be formed between the containers. To unmold, dip the outer container in hot water and swirl hot water around the inner container. You will then be able to separate the containers and leave a free-standing ice mold. Level off the bottom of the mold so it will stand without tipping. Place the mold in the freezer immediately. Fill with scoops of ice cream just before serving. (Serve the ice bowl on a tray lined with a white linen napkin because it melts fairly quickly. The tray will catch the drips.)

Put bowls of fruit or fruit salad on the table along with containers of chopped nuts, sugar cookies, a high stack of ice-cream cones, serving utensils, ice water, and espresso coffee.

⚹ ICE CREAM ⚹

Many, many procedures in the kitchen follow the same pattern. There is a basic plan and many variations. Thus the vanilla ice cream can become strawberry, chocolate, mocha, peach, blackberry, pistachio, or any other flavor you can devise. The underlying plan is to make a custard by cooking together a precise combination of ingredients: 4 cups of milk or cream, 4 egg yolks, 1 tablespoon of flour, and 1 cup of sugar. The custard when frozen becomes ice cream. In order to flavor the custard, vanilla is added *or* part of the milk is replaced with puréed fruit or fruit juice, melted chocolate, melted caramel, coffee, or nuts. Liqueurs can also be added but very sparingly, because the alcohol lowers the temperature at which the ice cream will freeze, and too much alcohol will inhibit solid freezing completely.

⤳ HOW TO MAKE ICE CREAM ⤶

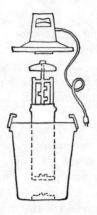

Ice cream is made at home, not because it is an economical thing to do, but because it is an inspired and beautiful thing to do. The first time it seems to take forever and you keep wondering why on earth you did not just go to the supermarket and buy some. But after the second or third batch it seems quite easy and relatively effortless. Homemade ice cream, brimming with fresh, ripe, pure fruit flavor nestled in sweet cream and eggs, richness begetting richness is a sensual delight of incomparable ecstasy. This is how to go about it.

1. When you unpack your new ice-cream freezer, read the manufacturer's directions. This instruction can reasonably be applied to other circumstances, but as reasonable as it sounds, it is a suggestion that is frequently scorned.

2. Prepare the ice-cream mixture and pour it into the can. Do not fill the can more than two thirds full or the top part will not freeze.

3. Crush the ice finely. Finely crushed ice produces a smooth, creamy texture to the ice cream.

4. Alternate 3 layers of crushed ice with coarse salt no more than a single layer in thickness. Too much salt causes the ice to freeze in blocks and alters the texture of the ice cream. The ice and salt should be 2″ in height above the level of the top of the ice cream in the can. You will need at least 1 large bag of ice and 1 cup of coarse salt.

5. Plug the ice-cream maker into an electric outlet and churn for approximately 20 minutes or until the motor sounds tired. Spoon the ice cream into freezer containers and place in the freezer until solidly frozen.

VANILLA ICE CREAM

MAKES 1½ QUARTS

4 cups light cream, or 2 cups milk   ¾ cup sugar
   and 2 cups whipping cream   ¼ teaspoon salt
4 egg yolks   1 tablespoon vanilla extract

Heat 2 cups of the cream or milk to simmering point. In the meantime stir together the egg yolks, sugar, and salt. Pour the simmering milk onto the egg yolk mixture and return to the saucepan. Stir continuously over low heat until the custard has thickened slightly. Do not let it boil. Remove from the heat and stir in the remaining cream or milk. Add the vanilla extract.

Cool the mixture and pour into the freezer can.

COMMENT: This quantity of ice cream fits into a standard ice-cream maker. To adapt it for the small machine that fits directly into the freezer, cut the recipe in half.

CHOCOLATE ICE CREAM

MAKES 1½ QUARTS

4 egg yolks   ¼ cup water
½ cup sugar   3½ cups light cream, or 1½ cups
¼ cup water   milk and 2 cups whipping cream
6 ounces sweet or semisweet
   chocolate

Beat the egg yolks in an electric mixer until thick and light in color. Put the sugar in a small heavy saucepan. Add the water and stir over low heat until the sugar has dissolved. Boil the syrup until it reaches 218° on a candy thermometer. The syrup will be extremely hot, so be very careful. Continue beating the egg yolks and add the boiling syrup *very* slowly in a continuous fine stream of drops. Continue beating at high speed. The eggs and syrup will triple in quantity.

In the meantime place the chocolate in a small saucepan. Add the remaining ¼ cup of water and stir over low heat until the chocolate has just melted. Stir the melted chocolate and the cream into the egg yolk mixture. Pour into the freezer can.

MOCHA ICE CREAM

Prepare chocolate ice cream (above) but substitute 1 cup of the milk or cream for 1 cup of triple strength coffee (3 teaspoons of instant coffee to 1 cup of boiling water). Add 2 tablespoons of coffee liqueur if you wish.

CHOCOLATE CHIP ICE CREAM

Prepare the vanilla ice cream (see Index). Break 6 ounces of semi-sweet or sweet chocolate into small pieces and put on a plate suspended over a pan of simmering water. Cover with another plate. Maintain over low heat until the chocolate has melted.

Line a baking sheet with wax paper and spread the chocolate over the paper in a thin layer using a metal spatula. Place in the freezer for 10 minutes until the chocolate is cold and brittle. Crumple the paper and the chocolate will break into tiny pieces. Stir the chocolate chips into the completed vanilla ice cream. Place in the freezer until solidly frozen.

STRAWBERRY, RASPBERRY, BLACKBERRY, OR OTHER BERRY ICE CREAM

Prepare the mixture for vanilla ice cream, using 2 cups cream only.

Purée 2 cups of berries in the blender and force the purée through a strainer to remove the seeds. Replace the remaining 2 cups of cream in the recipe with the fruit purée.

Cool the mixture and pour into the freezer can.

COMMENT: Fruit-flavored ice creams are improved in appearance with the addition of 4 or 5 drops of food coloring.

BUTTER PECAN ICE CREAM

Prepare the vanilla ice cream (see Index). Add 1 cup finely chopped pecans, 4 tablespoons melted butter, and ½ cup pure maple syrup.

COMMENT: Chop the nuts finely or they may become wedged between the dasher and the sides of the freezer can and prevent the dasher from turning.

PISTACHIO ICE CREAM

Prepare the vanilla ice cream (see Index). Add 1 cup ground pistachio nuts, 1 teaspoon almond extract, and 4 drops green food coloring.

STRAWBERRY SHERBET

Sherbet and ice cream are easy to make in the small ice-cream makers that fit in the freezer. Other berries may be substituted for the strawberries.

FOR 6

1 cup water	2 tablespoons lemon juice
¾ cup sugar	6 tablespoons Cointreau
1 quart strawberries	

Place the water and sugar in a small saucepan. Bring slowly to boiling point and boil gently for 5 minutes. Remove from the heat. Purée the strawberries in a blender and strain to remove the seeds. Add the strawberry purée and lemon juice to the syrup. Cool and place in the ice-cream maker or pour into 2 9″ layer-cake pans. Place in the freezer. Stir sherbet in the cake pan vigorously every hour until it is thick. Transfer to individual parfait dishes. Insert a chopstick or similar implement into the center of the sherbet and fill the hole with Cointreau or other fruit-flavored liqueur.

MELBA SAUCE

MAKES 1 CUP

1 cup raspberries
¼ cup superfine sugar

1 teaspoon lemon juice

Purée all the ingredients in the blender. Force through a fine strainer to remove the seeds.

COMMENT: Other berry sauces are made in the same way. Orange juice or fruit-flavored liqueur may be substituted for the lemon juice. If you would like a thicker sauce, pour the purée into a small saucepan. Heat to simmering point. Dissolve 2 teaspoons cornstarch in 1 tablespoon cold water and add to the sauce. Stir until thickened.

BUTTERSCOTCH SAUCE

MAKES 1¼ CUPS

2 cups brown sugar
¾ cup whipping cream
4 tablespoons butter

⅛ teaspoon salt
1 teaspoon vanilla extract

Place the sugar, cream, butter, and salt in a small, heavy saucepan. Set over low heat, stir occasionally until the sugar has dissolved, and simmer for 20 minutes until thick. Stir in the vanilla.

HOT FUDGE SAUCE

MAKES 1 CUP

6 ounces semisweet chocolate
2 tablespoons butter
¼ cup water

¼ cup sugar
½ cup whipping cream
1 teaspoon vanilla extract

Place the chocolate, butter, and water in a small, heavy saucepan. Place over low heat and stir until the chocolate has melted. Add the sugar and cream and simmer for 15 minutes. Remove from the heat and stir in the vanilla.

INDEX

R